C/26

D0828938

Linda Fortune

The House in Tyne Street

Childhood Memories of District Six

KWELA

The publisher and the author wish to acknowledge their sincere gratitude to

 Spier Management (Pty) Ltd, Stellenbosch
for its generous subsidy, which has made it possible to bring this
book on the market at such an affordable price;

G H Ally, Cloete Breytenbach, *Die Burger*, Colin de Vos, Noor Ebrahim,
J H Greshoff, George Hallett, Jimi Matthews and the Schroeder family, for
kindly granting us permission to reproduce their photographs.

The cover photograph of Eaton Place was taken by J H Greshoff in the early seventies
when the demolition of District Six was already in progress;

The photograph on the title page was taken by Jimi Matthews in 1971 at age 17, with
a camera given to him by his father, writer James Matthews. The half-demolished
double storey used to be in Tyne Street, facing Parkin Street, and from it pigeons
were raced and koeksisters sold;

The photographs appearing in the text are from the private collection of the author.

Copyright © 1996 Linda Fortune c/o Kwela Books
a division of NB Publishers, (Pty) Limited
40 Heerengracht, Cape Town
P.O. Box 6525, Roggebaai 8012.
http://www.kwela.com

All rights reserved.
No part of this book may be reproduced or transmitted in any
form or by any means, electronic, electrostatic, magnetic
tape or mechanical, including photocopying, recording, or by
any information storage and retrieval system, without
written permission of the publisher.

ISBN-10: 0-7957-0026-1
ISBN-13: 978-0-7957-0026-2

I wish to thank
my beloved sister Sheila Gangat Rolls, for all her dedication and
hard work in helping me;
my husband Des Fortune, for his support and encouragement;
my children Ryan, Deslyn and Kevin, who spurred me on by nagging,
"Mom, when are you going to finish your book?"
I dedicate this book to them.

The memories in it are also dedicated to
my brothers George, Roland, Roger and Jeff,
and to my sisters Pamela (Jordan) and Joan (Dawson),
with a special dedication to the memory of our parents, George
Alexander Gangat and Joan Elizabeth Gangat, and our Aunty
(Sissy) Helen Cornelius.

To protect their and other's privacy, I have changed most of the
names in these recollections of District Six. I have taken the liberty
to imagine conversations where I could not remember them exactly.
I have tried, however, not to distort any facts.

My sincere appreciation to
the Trustees and Members of the District Six Museum Foundation,
for their interest and encouragement,
and to the following people who kindly agreed to have photographs
either taken by them or in their possession to be used in my book:
G H Ally, Cloete Breytenbach, *Die Burger*, Colin de Vos, Noor
Ebrahim, J H Greshoff, George Hallett, Jimi Matthews and the
Schroeder family;
as well as to Annari van der Merwe and Nazli Jacobs, the editor and
the designer of this book.

Linda Fortune
March 1996

Contents

Thoughts

I HAD JUST COMPLETED READING an article about District Six in the Argus when suddenly I was overwhelmed with tremendous sadness.

I was all by myself in my own home and had nothing really to feel so sad about. It was a lovely day, a gentle breeze was blowing, the machine slowly tumbling the washing. The canaries in the cage on the patio were singing sweetly, our two puppies had just discovered that they could reach up into the plum tree and pull down the low-hanging branches so heavily laden with fruit. In the distance, turtle doves were making soft murmuring sounds. It was peaceful all around and yet I was feeling sad. Memories of our childhood home had come flooding back yet again and now I could not get District Six out of my mind.

I did not want to leave the way my family were forced to do in December 1971. At the time I wanted to plant my one foot on Devil's Peak and the other on Table Mountain and shout, "Let us stay, don't force us to go. You are destroying our families and our lives!"

But who would have listened? Nothing could be done. It was hopeless. We were helpless.

I must finally do something to ease my aching heart, I decided then and there. I must bury the past and get this feeling of hopelessness out of my system once and for all.

The best way to do it, I thought, would be to record what I remember and so preserve the once dearly loved place, a place which has ceased to exist but which will forever live in our hearts and our minds. That is how I came to tell the story of my family, our neighbours and our friends who once upon a time lived in a place called District Six.

1 The house in Tyne Street

WE LIVED IN A SEMI-DETACHED house facing Aspeling Street. On the other side of the wall, with his family, Mr A B Mitchel lived, and next to them, Boeta Bruima and Motjie Awa. Right opposite our house was an Indian babbie shop. Mr Gihwala, the proprietor, was known to all as Kika.

When you stepped out of our front door and looked to your right, you saw Hanover Street, and also Table Mountain.

Eleven people lived in our house in Tyne Street. They were my father Alex, my mother Jean, Aunty, my three sisters, Shirley, Patsy

A house in Tyne Street

and Daisy, and my four brothers, Ron, Pete, Jimmy and Colin – and myself, whom I will call Penny in this book.

The house had a flat roof with a parapet wall so that the corrugated roof sheets were not visible from the street. We had only one window facing the street, a long sash window mostly covered with brown wooden shutters. The bottom half of the house was painted the same brown colour, and the top half was whitewashed. Every year around Christmas time a fresh coat of whitewash would be applied.

Above the front door was a fanlight which always had a small white lace curtain drawn across it. Lower down on the door was a brass plate marked "LETTERS". When the postman put the letters through the letter slot, you could hear them fall onto the linoleum in the passage.

A long, wide passage ran from the front door to the kitchen. Two big rooms led off it, both to the left. At the end of the passage one step led down into the large kitchen, and the kitchen door opened onto the backyard.

The backyard was like part of the house. My father had installed a large off-white porcelain basin under the cold-water tap close to the kitchen door, and here all our washing was done. The washing lines were strung up from wall to wall.

In the far left-hand corner was the toilet. In the summer months a big galvanised bath would be placed in the toilet and we would bath there. In winter the bath would be carried into the kitchen or one of the rooms and used there. It always took two people to carry the bath filled with water.

There was also a small shed in the backyard. When the snoek was volop my dad would smoke some in the shed. He would put two primus stoves inside a long wooden box. Before lighting the stoves he would cover the tops with a metal sheet and sprinkle it with sawdust. On top of this a special grill with the well-salted fish was put. Once the flames had been turned low, the lid of the box was closed.

The shed also served as a hen house where our chickens laid their eggs and roosted at night.

A wooden gate with a big barrel bolt led onto the service lane behind our house. When the galvanised bath was not in use, it hung from a large hook on the gate.

Dad kept a number of old paraffin tins filled with soil in the back. Here he grew tomatoes, while Aunty pampered a row of pot-plants on the wide window sill that jutted out into the backyard – geraniums, ferns and fancy-leaves.

Mom and Aunty had been living in this house at number 14 Tyne Street since they were babies. They were both orphans and were adopted by a couple who had no children of their own. Mr and Mrs Hendricks lived quite happily in this house, bringing up the two little girls. Mom and Aunty told us many times that they gave them a very good life. Both girls were pretty and were brought up like ladies. They knew nothing about their past or about who had left them in the orphanage, not even if they were real sisters. The only family they ever knew was their adoptive mother and father. When the girls were in their twenties, both the parents died, and once again they were orphaned.

Aunty got married a short while later to Johnny Cornelius, a railway worker from Woodstock. But the marriage did not last and soon the two girls were once again alone in the world and in the house where they grew up. So they turned the front room into a sitting room and shared the back bedroom.

In the meantime the Second World War had ended, and my mother met a handsome young man who had just returned from the North after serving with the Union Defence Forces. He was the proud owner of a letter signed by General Smuts, the then Minister of Defence, thanking him and his comrades for the part

3

they had played in "this great world struggle". The letter was dated July 31, 1945 and addressed to No M 14659V WS/L/Cpl, followed by his full name.

My mother and father got married and moved into the back room, and Aunty moved into the sitting room. The three shared the rest of the house. This was still how it was when we children were small.

First Ron was born, and then I. Shirley was born a year later and for about five years it was just the three of us. It was lovely being just three children. We got the best of everything. Besides, Aunty was like a second mother to us. But then things started to change, and in the end we were eight children. Aunty spent more and more time in her room as she could not handle the noise of the children. The house was just too small for all of us and we all got on each other's nerves.

2 Our street

WE LIVED IN TYNE STREET – known by the people of District Six as "Tiny" Street. My mother used to say to my father that it was no use trying to change the way we or the people of District Six spoke as we were all set in our ways. So to this day the people would say Tiny Street, even though it does not exist any more.

At the top of Tyne Street were two famous District Six shops: Shrand's shoe shop, and on the opposite corner, Van der Schyff's dress material shop. Shrand's sold the very latest in fashion shoes and the very best quality. Van der Schyff's stocked the most beautiful materials for wedding gowns and bridesmaids' dresses.

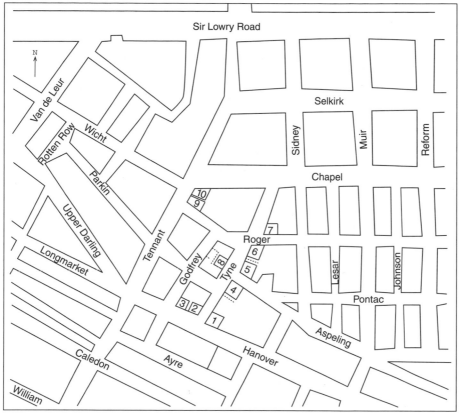

1 Van der Schyff's   2 Shrand's   3 Rooikop Jood   4 Kika's   5 Adam's
6 The Building   7 Kader's   8 Number 14   9 Mr L A Guma   10 Solly's

Besides these two fancy shops we also had two babbie shops. Kika's was on the corner of Aspeling and Tyne Streets, and Mr Kader's on the corner of Roger and Tyne Streets. If one shop did not have an item in stock, it was never a problem because it took you less than a minute to walk to the other.

All the shopkeepers in our neighbourhood were very hardworking. The shops would be open from before seven in the morning till late in the evening. During the hot summer months they would stay open till even later at night to sell cold drinks and frozen suckers.

Not many people in District Six owned refrigerators so perishables were bought as they were needed. Sometimes my dad would ask the shopkeeper to store some fish or crayfish in his fridge for him. The shopkeeper would never refuse and Dad always saw to it that the man got a fair share of whatever he had stored.

Telephones were similarly shared. We would ask the shopkeeper if we could please use the phone. Permission was granted only if it was an emergency. The motjie always asked the number and when you had given it, this Muslim or Indian lady shopkeeper would dial it herself – just in case you wanted to make a long distance call after all.

The shopkeepers were nice but they never trusted anybody.

In the early days we still used "English" money: pounds, shillings and pennies. Rands and cents came only later. And a sixpence – six pennies – was a lot of money to us children. Even a tickey – three pennies – made us feel rich, though it was worth more or less one cent when they later changed the currency!

Most people were paid weekly and earned very little and lived from hand to mouth, so the babbie would sell any small quantity to a regular customer. You could buy a tickey's worth of jam, peanut butter, vinegar, blue soap or washing powder. One could buy one loose sheet of greaseproof paper, one cigarette and even one egg. "Star" sweets were huge and were sold three for a penny.

On very special occasions, like the opening of a new shop, a birthday of one of his children, or the return of one of the family from a pilgrimage to Mecca, a babbie would send a fresh loaf of bread to all the families on the street to show his appreciation to them for buying from him. It was believed that such generosity would bring him luck.

6

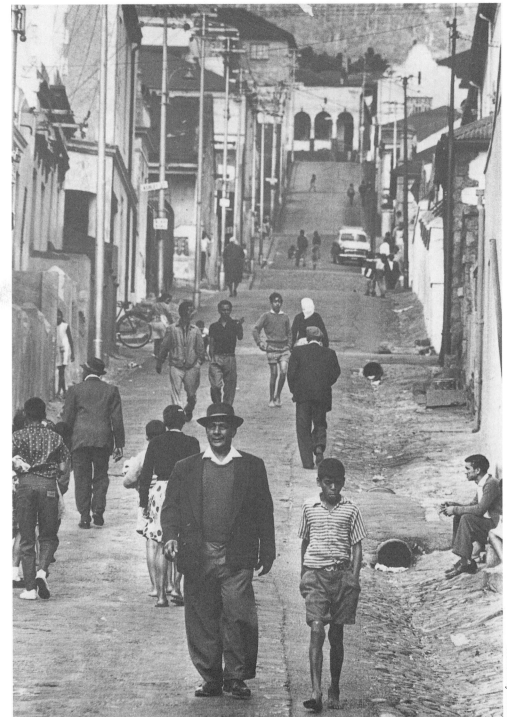

Cloete Breytenbach

J H Greshoff

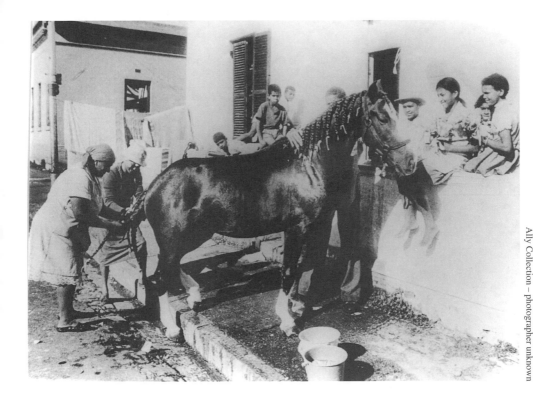

Ally Collection – photographer unknown

Previous page: Richmond Street in the sixties, with Table Mountain vaguely discernable in the background. Due to the size of the houses and the lack of private gardens and public parks, life happened on the street as much as indoors. As a result no secrets could be kept and people usually far outnumbered vehicles.

Facing page: The typical interior of a semi-detached house. The long passage, where lace curtains, seldom drawn, could shield the intimate scene in the small, compact kitchen at the end, was found in most houses. Front doors were seldom locked, and neighbours and friends rarely knocked.

Above: Just about everything happened on the street. A horse, which would have been kept in a stable somewhere at the back of a house, is being groomed for some special occasion, while the children of the neighbourhood look on approvingly and appreciatively.

Next page: Washing had to be dried wherever there was space: up in the air - strung up in front of the Standard Building in Hanover Street in this case - or down on the pavement. If people were lucky they had a small backyard where their wet things could dry out of the public eye.

J H Greshoff

In between the shops there were ordinary houses.

My mother told us that Mr Mitchel, our neighbour at number 12, was the captain of one of the most famous carnival troupes of the District, "The Cape Town Hawkers". We never knew if he was responsible, but every New Year's Eve, lengths of satin material were hung from the top of the electric poles along our street for all to see.

The shiny satin made our street look so pretty. Walking up Tyne Street from the Chapel Street end, looking straight ahead, you could see the different-coloured streamers stretching from one end of the street to the other. It was a fantastic sight with Table Mountain majestic and proud in the background, as if saying, "Well done, my troupies, your colours are perfect!"

Now and then a gentle breeze would make the streamers flutter to remind people that it was New Year in District Six.

Across from our house lived a Muslim family: a father, a mother and eight grown-up children – five sisters and three brothers. They were a very happy bunch and everybody in the street thought them a lovely family. The father, Mr Adams, was a quiet person, tall and slender, always wearing a red fez with a tassel which hung to the side. The mother and the children were very modern and fashionable. Sometimes they would give a party to celebrate a birthday. At such times they played Elvis music and wore stovepipes and sweaters and soft black kid-glove shoes. Whenever my sister Shirley and I heard the wild music we would sneak out of our house quietly, and go and peer through their front-room window to watch them dance. When it was fast music, some party-goers did the "rock'n'roll" while others did the "bop". When the lights were switched off later and the girls moved closer to their partners to shuffle to the soft, slow music playing on the gramophone, Shirley and I, about ten at the time, would giggle.

Much later we learned that this dance that one did in the dark was called the "blues".

Rachmat was my favourite of the Adams sisters, because when it was dennebolpitjietyd she used to pop the pine cones into the oven and call me over to their house. One of her brothers would go up to De Waal Drive, just above the District, to collect bags full of cones under the huge old pine trees on the Table Mountain side of the road.

When the pine cones started bursting open from the heat, it meant that they could be removed from the oven. Rachmat would spread newspaper on the stoep and the two of us would crack open the pine kernels with a hammer or a stone, remove the pips and pop them into our mouths. It was delicious.

3 Dad

DAD WAS AN UPHOLSTERER and motor trimmer while Mom stayed home to take care of us. Dad worked at the same place most of his life. In his free time, he often did private work at home, "spare work" as we called it: re-upholstering people's car seats, replacing the carpeting, the hood linings, door panelling and arm rests. He was very good at what he did. He had a big industrial sewing machine at home and many times Mom, Ron and I had to help him by holding the car seats while he fitted the covers. He taught me how to use this big machine and soon I helped him with the sewing of the heavy covers although I must have been only about twelve years old. It was hard work. Ron and I spent many of our weekends helping him. While the other children played, we had to work. We didn't always think it was fair.

As Ron grew older, Dad taught him everything he knew about his trade and as soon as Ron left school, he took him along to his place of work. The two of them worked at the same place in Roeland Street for a few years.

While Dad continued with his spare work, Ron developed other interests. He belonged to the St Mark's Judo Club and the Cape Province Mountain Club. In the end he did not have time to help Dad any longer, but Dad did not seem to mind. He encouraged him to go on with his sports. He even made Ron's judo suit. He also bought him a genuine mountaineering haversack, thick woollen socks, mountaineering boots, a sleeping bag and a thick blue outdoor jacket with many pockets. And so with Ron out and about and not being able to help Dad, and me too busy with my school work, Dad started Pete off to help him with his spare work. Pete was quite interested and when he later left school, he too took up the trade of upholsterer.

When Dad was not busy with spare work in his bedroom – the only place where he could do it – he went crayfishing. Sometimes in the middle of the week, early in the morning before work, he'd set out. His favourite place was Oudekraal, and sometimes Fourth Beach at Clifton. He knew all the best spots and only went when the tide and the moon were right. Sometimes in summer he would get up even before it got light to catch the very first bus to Bakoven, just beyond Camps Bay, and from there walk the three miles along the coastal road to Oudekraal, catch his crayfish and hottentot fish and return home with a laden bag. He would get cleaned up and then go to work.

At that time there were no such things as crayfish restrictions. You could go and catch anywhere and as many as you wanted. Dad only brought home the biggest crayfish. He always threw back the small ones and the females with "berries" on them – tiny red eggs attached to the underside of their tails.

Dad had great respect for the sea.

Many times he would take the three of us older children along, and often other youngsters from the neighbourhood were also included in the crayfish outing. Dad must have looked like the Pied Piper of Hamelin, with up to eight children trailing behind him! His usual fishing outfit consisted of a long-sleeved khaki shirt, old pants and a jacket, thick rubber-soled shoes and a khaki canvas haversack for carrying eatables and bottles of fresh water for drinking. Some of the bigger children had their own bags.

Before we set off, Dad would line up all the children at the front door and count them. He would then split them into two groups and the two biggest children in each group were told to take care of the smaller ones. If the bus conductor asked him whether the children were all his, Dad would say yes.

He loved his drink and when he went on his fishing trips, he always filled his old army bottle with "medicine" and slung it over his shoulder. The bus conductor on the Camps Bay and Bakoven route and he got to know each other so well that he often offered the man a shot from his "water bottle".

Dad was a very strict father and discipline was his top priority. Children had to obey their parents. Rudeness was not tolerated. Mom, on the other hand, was soft. She hardly ever gave us a hiding. When she could not handle us, she used to say, "I see that you don't want to listen to me, don't say that I didn't warn you."

She did not always tell Dad, as she threatened, but if it was something serious you could prepare yourself for the worst: Dad's army belt. He would fold the wide leather strap double, take you over his knee and smack your bottom a few times. This hurt terribly, but the humiliation of getting a hiding was worse than the physical pain.

Sometimes when he was really upset or in a bad mood, Dad would hit hard and go on hitting. Then, when Mom thought it was enough, she would intervene and stop him. She sometimes cried when he beat us. Most times he would come to us afterwards and explain why he had to punish us. He said it did not give him pleasure and it hurt him too, but it was because he loved us and it was a father's duty to discipline his children.

As we grew bigger, Dad grew older and did not beat us any more – instead we had to write lines. The writing took a lot of time, whereas a hiding was over quickly. We could not always decide which we preferred. One day my youngest brother, Colin, did something wrong, I don't remember what. Dad was sick at the time and Colin had to write out twenty-five times: "I must obey my parents at all times."

Colin, who was about seven, went to Dad and said, "Dad, here's the belt, give me six of the best, then I don't have to write all those lines. It is too much writing for a little boy like me. Look, I got short fingers and it'll take me a year to write so many lines."

Dad was highly amused, but said sternly, "Colin, take your punishment like a man, and go and write those lines."

4   Our Aunty

S HE WAS AN EXTROVERT and followed no rules. She had black hair and wore spectacles. She was attractive, very talented and she always had a slim figure. People said I looked like her.

Aunty Iris was her name but everybody called her just plain old "Aunty". Like my mother, she had been living in that house in Tyne Street all of her life. She stayed in the front room all by herself while the rest of us, ten in total, were crammed into the back

11

Aunty with Ron as a baby

room and the passage. Hers was a very big room.

Aunty's husband left her just before Mom married Dad. She never had children, my mother said, because she "did something" when she was young and it had "messed her up". None of us ever asked what she did and nobody discovered the reason why her husband one day just packed up and went back to live with his mother in Woodstock, never divorcing her.

Every end of the month Aunty took me with her to Woodstock. We boarded a bus down in Sir Lowry Road next to the Castle and got out in Albert Street, near Woodstock Station. She always waited on the corner of the street where her husband lived and sent me to collect her money. He paid her maintenance till the day she died.

The money was always ready in an envelope, and I always got half-a-crown from Aunty Mary, the old lady who also lived in the house. The two-and-six made me feel very rich. I would clutch the coin in my hand, stand around a bit, and when I thought I had stayed long enough, I would greet the tall, well-built man and his old mother politely, and run back to the corner to meet Aunty.

I never saw Uncle Johnny without his hat on.

I could not understand these two grown-ups. He gave her money every month, but they never ever spoke one word to each other.

12

Aunty and I would then wait in Albert Road for a bus back to town. We never went straight home. Instead we stayed on the bus until it reached the terminus opposite the Post Office, next to the Parade. First Aunty would go to the chemist in Plein Street called the Nitekem, and make her purchase of asthma tablets, Palmolive soap and shampoo, Vaseline, Vicks, Kleenex tissues and Mum deodorant, which came in a little round, red container. Aunty liked nice things and was rather fussy. Then she would lead me across to the Parade where she bought dried fruit, peanuts and sweets.

Our shopping completed, we did not take a bus home because it only took us ten minutes to walk up the gentle slope to Tyne Street. The moment we got home, the rest of the children gathered in Aunty's room, eager for her to start dishing out her fruit and sweets. They always wanted to know how much money I'd been given in Woodstock, but I wouldn't say because I thought to myself that if I could wait till the next day, I would go and buy that toy tea set from Mr Goodman's shop at the top of Hanover Street. I would take only Shirley with me. The tea set cost two bob – two shillings – and I would still get sixpence change. I would spend a tickey on sweets for myself, and the tickey that was left, I would give to Shirley.

Aunty gave me my first knitting lesson. She handed me two long thick steel nails and a piece of wool, showed me how to put stitches on the nails, and then actually how to knit. I was told to practise and promised that as soon as I had mastered the technique of knitting, she would give me my own real knitting needles and two balls of pink wool.

She did. I finished a pink scarf and she encouraged me to carry on knitting. She was a very good knitter and made all our jerseys. Sometimes she took on orders to knit for the neighbours and her friends. They had to supply their own wool and patterns and she charged them by the ounce – two shillings for double or triple knit, and half-a-crown for four-ply wool.

Aunty was very temperamental. There were days when she and my mother would be the very best of friends. Then there were times when they did not speak to each other for weeks. Most of their quarrels were over us children. Aunty was a person who liked to sleep, and the noise in the house disturbed her.

After school on rainy days we used to play near the hallstand in the passage outside her door. Whenever we made a noise she got out of her bed and stormed at us, beating wildly at the lot of us with her slipper. Usually we managed to dash down the passage and stay out of her reach, but if she managed to grab hold of one of us she would hit that child all over, even across the face. Sometimes the slipper left red marks and when my dad questioned Mom in the evening about where these marks came from, she would tell him that we had fallen.

"Fallen, that's utter rubbish and you know it!" he would yell at Mom. "These kids were beaten by You-know-who. Why are you always protecting her? She doesn't deserve a sister like you and I'm warning you, if this happens again, I'll throw her out of this house. I swear."

I could never understand why Aunty was always sleeping, sometimes for days on end, and why my mother tried to keep us quiet as best she could. It was only as I grew older that I discovered that Aunty was taking pills. She called me one day and told me that she will never hit me again if I get her some of Dad's sleeping pills.

"I can't, Aunty," I said. "Dad will send me away to the convent if he catches me stealing the pills."

"Don't worry. Your dad goes to the doctor for regular check-ups. Every time he gets more pills. He'll never miss a few."

It was true that my dad had to have regular check-ups. Because of the Second World War. Aunty knew about the pills because my mother had told her that the doctor gave my dad pills each time as

14

he sometimes had trouble sleeping. He was always talking and thinking about the time he spent in the army.

"No, Aunty, I'm not going to steal the pills. I don't even know what they look like," I said and ran out of the house to look for my mother. I couldn't find her and when I went back inside, I heard a noise coming from my parents' room. I tiptoed down the passage and peeped round the door.

There was Aunty searching through all the drawers in the room. Next she searched Dad's jacket pockets. She found a small brown bottle of pills. She poured some into her hand but left the rest in the bottle. I was gone by the time she came out of the room.

As Aunty said, my dad never missed the pills. He hardly ever used them. He still had to go to the doctor regularly, and each time the doctor simply gave him another bottle. These he always put in his jacket pocket, and each time Aunty must have helped herself when nobody was around.

One day when I was alone at home I went to look for the pills she was so fond of. In the jacket pocket I discovered a few bottles. They all had cotton wool pressed down into them so that you wouldn't notice right away they were almost empty. Aunty never emptied a bottle completely.

Then one day, Dad brought the jacket to Mom and asked her to take it to the cleaners. "First empty the pockets and I'll send one of the children down to Nannucci Cleaners with it," she said.

Dad took all the bottles from the pocket. "Strange," he said, "I could've sworn there were more pills in these bottles. I might as well empty out all the bottles and throw the whole lot away."

Mom did not try to stop him. She only asked him why he didn't use them.

"They make me feel terrible the next morning, and I don't believe in taking sleeping pills anyway." So he went into the backyard and poured the pills down the drain and chucked the empty bottles into the bin.

Aunty happened to be in the yard. As she watched the whole procedure she dug her fingernails into the palms of her hands and opened her mouth to say something. But then she pressed her lips tightly together and walked away. There was nothing she could do.

I never told my mother any of this because I was too frightened Auntie would find out and hurt me.

Dad must have recovered from whatever he was troubled with, as he stopped going to the doctor. This also put a stop to Aunty's supply of pills. So she made another plan. She started telling the neighbours that she suffered from all kinds of sicknesses, and they began giving her their left-over pills. I asked Mom what was wrong with her, and why she was drinking all kinds of pills.

"She's a hypochondriac," Mom said.

Sometimes when the southeaster blew Aunty took a scarf and tied it around her face which she had rubbed full of Vicks. One never knew if she really suffered, or if she was just imagining it.

When Aunty was in one of her good moods, she used to invite Shirley and me into her room. We were allowed to sit on her bed and she would take out a jar of sweets and tell us stories about her and Mom's childhood, how they were orphaned twice, why she never left the house in Tyne Street to live somewhere else and how she now took it for granted that she was our "other mother".

Aunty told us that she had worked in a clothing factory for many years. She could cut a man's pants and sew them too.

"Before you were born, life in District Six was different," she said one day.

"What was so different?" we wanted to know.

"When your mom and I were young, there was no such a thing as apartheid. People could marry whomever they wished and live wherever they chose. Here in this neighbourhood there lived

16

Jewish, Indian, Native, Muslim, Christian and even Chinese people. They all got on well and we never had to lock our front doors at night. People lived freely, and they had a lot of respect for each other. Life started to change when people began to move away one by one. The houses were beginning to deteriorate. Then the landlords allowed just anybody to rent from them. Gangs appeared and suddenly there was a lot of crime going on."

Aunty was sitting at her dressing table, brushing her long, black hair with her pretty hairbrush.

"And then after the war, apartheid was introduced and the District started slipping downhill slowly but surely."

One of Aunty's favourite places used to be the pier down at Table Bay harbour. When she was young she and her friends would go there over the weekends, dancing to the music of the big bands. But after she got married and her husband left her, she never went dancing again.

She told us how she saw Queen Elizabeth and Princess Margaret when they paid a visit to Cape Town in 1947. She waved to them when they passed the City Hall.

As soon as Aunty got tired of us, she would send us away abruptly, and we had to wait for another good mood before she would continue her story telling.

In spite of Aunty's strange ways and moods, and even though she sometimes beat us, we all loved her. Mainly because she came to our rescue if the children in the street beat us up. She had a sharp tongue and was never afraid of anybody.

5 Washday

I T WAS A SATURDAY AFTERNOON. Warm sunlight filtered down onto the stone-paved backyard. Mom was doing the washing at the cold-water tap near the kitchen door. She was bent over the washing plank on the large off-white porcelain basin, soaping in and rubbing the white things – sheets and pillowcases and shirts and bits of underwear. Shirley and I were playing happily under an overturned wooden bench which Dad had made. Ron was playing somewhere in the house, or perhaps even in the street. When he was not around, Shirley and I had no problems, because he was always, as Mom put it, "interfering with the girls" and causing a hullabaloo.

Then Mom rinsed the washing, pulling each piece out of the clean water with two hands, dropping it back again and pulling it out again until she was sure it was properly rinsed. She hung it up on the washing lines which ran from one end of the yard to the other. She took the washing plank and quickly pushed it underneath the middle washing line to prevent it from sagging to the ground.

Playtime was over, unless we wanted to be soaked by the dripping water, because when Mom hung up her washing it was always sopping wet and it would soak everything in the yard. Mom could not twist the wet washing like the other women in the District did. She just sort of squeezed the water out, so when she hung the sheets up they were still heavy with water.

Shirley and I giggled.

"What's tickling you two?" Mom wanted to know.

We said it was nothing, but we whispered to each other, "When Dora comes to help with the washing the water doesn't drip from

18

the clothes and we don't have to leave the yard to play outside in the street."

When the wet washing drove us into the street, we never had a shortage of friends.

"What next?" I would say and Shirley always suggested immediately, "Drie blikkies."

"Okay," I would shout, "I'll get the tennis ball."

But I could never find it. I'd scream, "Mom, where's the ball? We want to play drie blikkies."

"You know your dad does not want you girls playing in the street," she'd reply.

"Oh, please, Mom, tell me where it is."

"Okay, go and look under my bed," she'd say, "but don't play for too long, and don't get yourselves dirty. I don't want your father to blame me every time you children do wrong."

In the meantime Shirley was rounding up some friends whose task it was to find three empty tins. This was easy. All you needed to do was go to the nearest service lane, dig through the garbage, and the choice was yours.

My favourite tins were the All Gold two-pound apricot jam tins because they were bigger than the condensed milk ones, and it was easier to throw the ball at them.

Drie blikkies could be played by up to ten children. Three tins were balanced one on top of the other. A pitcher would then throw the tennis ball at the tins as hard as she could, trying to scatter them as far as possible. The other kids now had to place the tins one on top of the other again, but without being "tagged" by the pitcher who would throw the ball at them, trying to eliminate them from the game by hitting them. The pitcher had three chances to hit the tins. If she missed each time, it was someone else's turn.

No matter how much we enjoyed playing in the street, it was

always in the back of my mind that Dad did not want us to play there. So, a few runs up and down and about and then I'd shout, "Game's over! Our dad's going to come down the road any moment now."

Immediately tins would go flying back into the lane, and the ball under the bed. Time to wash and comb our hair.

When Dad came home, we looked real innocent.

6 Games and little friends

THERE WAS NEVER A SHORTAGE of children to play with in Tyne Street or anywhere else in District Six. If your sisters or brothers did not want you around, all you had to do was go outside and join the first group of children. You would be included and no questions asked.

The girls had their own games and rules, and the boys had theirs. Girls and boys hardly ever played together.

Besides playing hide-and-seek and hopscotch and skipping rope the girls loved games like house-house, shop-shop, school-school and phone-phone.

For house-house, each little girl would bring out her rag or rubber doll and parade up and down the pavement, rocking it to and fro in her arms, just like her mommy did at home with the little ones.

Dressing up in your mom's clothes was also part of playing house-house. For this purpose the mothers would give their little daughters old hats, high-heeled shoes, handbags, gloves, and dresses they didn't wear any more. A string of cheap pearls, secretly borrowed, and a dash of lipstick across the lips were all part of the dressing up.

The girls also play-played at cooking food. Pieces of wood from a tomato box that the bigger boys had brought home from the market in Sir Lowry Road were piled up outside on the pavement under the sash window with the wooden shutters. An empty jam tin was put on top and wilted pieces of cabbage, carrot leaves and potato peels – fetched from the kitchen where Mom was busy cleaning the vegetables – were put inside. The jam tin was then filled with water from another tin which served as a jug. In a few short minutes the food, cooked over a fire that was never lit, would be dished up with a piece of plank and "spooned" onto toy plastic plates. Each little girl would pretend to eat and enjoy her helping of food.

To play shop-shop, money was needed. For paper money old newspapers were torn into small pieces and folded up to look like pound notes. Pieces of glass were used for small change. Small empty boxes were sold as Joko tea, Eleven O'Clock rooibos tea, jelly and St Moritz cigarettes. Small empty tins were sold as Royal baking powder or Nespray baby milk, which was of course needed for the baby dolls.

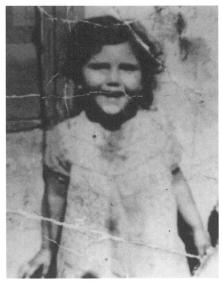

Penny at age 5

School-school was another favourite, especially imitating primary school teachers doing a lice inspection. The younger girls had heard about this frightful event from playmates who already went to school or from their older brothers and sisters. So one little girl would line the others up, take two sticks to part the hair of the girls in her "class" and each time say, "Your hair is full of goggas. Go and tell your mother to come and see me at the school."

The telephones used in phone-phone were made from two empty tins and a long piece of string. A father or an older brother would be asked to make a hole in the bottom of one tin, put the string through it from the outside and fasten it inside. In the same way he would attach the other end of the string to the second tin. You then talked into the tin, pretending to be speaking to a friend or neighbour. In those days children used anything to play with. Especially tins and ordinary pebbles.

Charms was a lovely game, but it was a bit expensive and sometimes led to tears. To be able to play it you had to own charms, and these you couldn't just pick up or make. You had to buy them. At that time, the OK Bazaars sold Lucky Packets, and inside those with "For Girls" written on the outside were sweets and a few plastic charms. The charms came in all different colours and shapes – small animals, fishes, ballerinas, mermaids, horses, birds or hats. Armed with these pretty treasures, which could also be worn on a piece of string or chain around your neck or arm, two girls would play charms.

A circle was drawn on the pavement with a stone, and a few feet away a starting line was marked off. Now each girl had to aim and throw her charm into the circle. If she missed the circle, she had one more chance to shoot the charm in with her index finger and thumb. If she missed again, she was out and it was her partner's turn to play.

Sometimes you lost all your charms and sometimes you won all your playmate's. Whoever lost would most times start crying and complain that the other one had cheated. She would insist on having her charms back and the other girl would swear that she'd never play with such a cry-baby again.

If both little girls were nice, they would share the charms out equally and start the game all over again.

The boys played games like "Jack be gun", cowboys and crooks, scooters, marbles, kennetjie, kites, kerem, dominoes, cricket, soccer and rugby. They played wild games and afterwards many of them had scraped knees and elbows. The girls stayed out of their way and watched from a distance. Except on Guy Fawkes day.

Each year on the fifth of November, the boys would make a dummy man from old broomsticks and dress it in old clothes. In the evening they carried this ugly creature around the neighbourhood and knocked on everyone's door asking for money for "the guy". Some people gave them a penny or two, but some would chase them away.

In District Six there must have been some kind of magic at work, because in some mysterious way the children always seemed to know exactly when it was time to change to games. One day everybody would be playing drie blikkies, Shirley's favourite, or cowboys and crooks, and the next day all the girls and all the boys would be playing a different game, as if some fairy had whispered the name of the new game in the little ones' ears the night before.

There was even a season that certain songs would suddenly be sung. Out of the blue all the girls would start singing:

Ten o'clock is striking, my ma won't let me out,
My young man is waiting, he wants to take me out.
He takes me round the corner, he takes me overseas,
He takes me to my uncle, to have a cup of tea.

If the boys ever heard the girls singing "My young man is waiting" they would hoot with laughter. They'd tease them and say we were old-fashioned. Where did we think anyone would still find a boyfriend that would be waiting for a girl? And would take her out for tea?

The boys always laughed when they saw girls playing their games, but they didn't like it if the girls dared to laugh at their games.

7 Going to school

WE WENT TO TWO DIFFERENT SCHOOLS before high school. From Sub A to Standard Two we attended the primary school in William Street, and from Standard Three to Standard Five we went to the junior school on the corner of Tennant Street.

The school in William Street was very nice. The classrooms were big with wooden floors that were always clean and shiny. Upstairs was a large gymnasium where we did physical training when the weather was bad. Otherwise we had to go outside.

After school the gymnasium was used by the community of District Six. Here you could take up judo, gymnastics, boxing, body building and other sporting activities.

Children starting school had to be registered well in advance, usually in the middle of the previous year. The mother and father, with the child's birth certificate safely tucked into the man's jacket pocket, would take the little one to the principal's office where the teacher on duty would fill in the necessary forms and ask all sorts of unnecessary questions. When it was Colin's turn, he was asked what he wanted to be when he grew up. He answered that he wanted to paint. The teacher didn't understand, so he whispered in Mom's ear, "Tell her about the man who sit by the pole outside the house, the old man that paint Table Mountain."

"Oh, you want to be an artist," the teacher said, bending down to his level.

"Yes," he replied, fiddling with his thumbs, "an artist." Then he looked up and asked, "Daddy, what's an artist?"

School was different then. For one, the children were fed at school. During the summer months the teachers would line us up in the playground during interval and hand out fruit to us. The boys in their short grey pants, white shirts and royal blue ties, and the girls in their navy blue gym slips, white shirts, royal blue girdles and ties, stood in separate queues. The teacher on duty would say, "Stretch and lower!" and we'd put our stretched-out hands on the shoulders of the child in front of us and then lower them so that there would be an equal distance between all of us.

Sometimes we got a bunch of grapes, or it would be an apple, orange, peach, or banana. It just depended on what was available. What I liked best of all was watermelon season when we each got a thick slice of juicy, sweet watermelon – even though the boys sometimes chased us with the peels, theatening to smear us, so that we shrieked and ran away in all directions. If the skin of the watermelon was really thick, we were asked to place it in a large container afterwards. The tea lady would clean the peels and turn them into watermelon konfyt. She cooked the konfyt in a large pot in the school kitchen. When it was ready, she used to put it in glass jars and share it out among the teachers.

In addition to the fruit, slices of brown bread, spread with either jam or peanut butter, were sent round to the classrooms every day. My brothers and sisters and I never helped ourselves to these as the bread was intended for those children who could not afford to bring sandwiches to school.

We also got milk every day, and this was for everybody; you just had to bring your own mug or cup. The milk was always nice and creamy. There were times when it was flavoured with strawberry syrup, which made it pink, so we called it "milkshake", something which few people in the district could afford. It was indeed a treat!

Once it was my eldest brother Ron and his friend Frankie's turn to collect the milk from the kitchen. The two of them carried the pail of strawberry milkshake to the classroom, where it was always shared out, and told their class that they had spat into it on their way. The other pupils were furious and refused to drink the milk, so Ron and Frankie could drink as much as they wanted. Only after they had enough did they say, "Listen, everyone, we didn't spit in the milk, honestly." Now the other children were really angry. In the end, some came up for their milk, but many did not.

Often a friend and I were told to collect the bread from the kitchen. If the tea lady was not around, I would look for the crust of the brown bread and spread it very thickly with the peanut butter. While I was busy with the bread, Jane would stand outside to warn me if the tea lady came in view. Fortunately for us we were never caught in the act.

We would then put our crusts, smothered in peanut butter, under the other slices of bread on the tray, and as the children took their slices we would reach for our special pieces. The others knew that these crusts were not meant for them. We'd go outside with everybody else to eat and showed off the way the peanut butter ran off the sides of our bread.

In winter the children who could afford it were asked each to bring a vegetable for soup. My Standard One teacher made the best soup in the school. She had a very big pot and primus stove at the back of the class. The prettiest girls in the class were always chosen to clean the vegetables. This meant that we did not have to do school work. Besides, while the rest of the class had to do silent reading, we sat around cleaning vegetables and listening to the teacher telling us stories about her life.

The vegetables had to be grated, and ever so often one of us would grate our fingers in the process. We never complained, because at that time, a school child would do anything to win the teacher's favour.

The pot of water and vegetables would be put on the primus and left to boil on a low heat until the next morning. Most of the time the soup was very tasty – except on days when the caretaker on duty forgot to check and stir the pot occasionally, and the soup was burnt. But that did not stop us from eating it! It was fun and sometimes if you were lucky you were given a nice juicy bone. The soup meat was supplied by a Muslim family whose daughter attended our school, because if the meat was not halaal, the Muslim children would not eat the soup, irrespective of how nice it smelt or tasted. They would rather go hungry.

I liked to be sent on an errand to the principal's office. In my eyes he was a very nice man because he always spoke so politely to us, and I don't remember ever being scared of him like some children were. He was a stout man and wore small round spectacles which made him look like an owl. He sat behind a neatly organised and always highly polished large brown desk. The walls were lined with book shelves full of books. On a corner shelf was a "ball" covered with the map of the world that could turn on its little stand. Usually, Mr Hendricks had a vase with flowers on the side of the desk.

Everyone respected the principal of our school. If all the teachers in our school in William Street were as kind and conscientious as him, the lot of us would possibly have turned out much brighter!

But the other teachers' favourite pastime was to hit the children. You were beaten with a cane for wearing the wrong clothes, for wearing the wrong colour ribbon in your hair. Even the colour and style of your shoes had to be perfect or you were beaten. Many of the families were poor and could not afford the school uniform, and some children came to school barefoot. But the teachers would not listen to reason and every time a child was not properly dressed, he or she got a beating.

Many times I silently prayed in class for a teacher to disappear down a crack in the floor boards, never to return. It wasn't the child's fault if he didn't have the right clothes or colours; why didn't the teacher go to that child's home to see for himself the conditions they lived under?

Quite a few children dropped out of school because of the teachers, and parents were too reluctant or ignorant to approach the teacher or the principal about the beatings.

8   My first beating at school

I WAS IN STANDARD TWO and it was the first term of school. I thought our teacher, Miss Fisher, was very nice. She had a lovely figure, a pretty face and wore smart clothes. I even thought that when I finished school I might become a teacher and look like her.

But then one morning I was daydreaming in class when she asked me a question. I could not answer because I hadn't been listening to what she said. I was scared.

"Stand up, Penny," she said. "Why don't you listen to me when I speak? What do you sit and dream about?"

I was embarrassed as the whole class was looking at me. Some girls giggled behind their hands. I was numb with fear and could not speak. I could feel my mouth getting dry and tears pricking behind my eyelids.

Miss Fisher jumped up and pushed me towards her desk where she reached for a wooden ruler. She took my right hand and closed it into a fist. She turned the ruler onto its side and hit me across the knuckles. She kept on hitting. In the end I pulled my hand away and looked at it. The knuckles were bleeding and swollen. I screamed, dashed through the door and ran away.

I didn't stop running until I reached home. Aunty was standing in the open front door. "What are you doing at home so early?" she asked.

I burst into tears. Sobbing I showed her my knuckles.

Aunty was shocked at what she saw. "Did you do something wrong?" she demanded. "Who did this to you?"

I told her that I was not paying attention when the teacher spoke and that she got angry when she questioned me and I could not answer.

Aunty didn't say anything. She just took me by the arm and marched me back to school.

"I'm never going back there. I want my mother," I wailed.

"Listen to me carefully, Penny," she said. "I don't want your mother to see you like this. Remember she is pregnant and the doctor said that she is almost on her last. We can't upset her right now. You know she has a very soft heart and will never go to the school to find out why you were beaten like this."

Still clutching my arm, Aunty continued, "I know what she will do. She'll clean up your hand and try and make it look better, and then tonight, when your father comes home from work, she'll first give him his supper and maybe then she'll tell him. So you see, Penny, my dear child, by then your hand won't look so bad and the swelling might be gone. Your dad might even say that you deserved what you got for not paying attention. So this is why I'm taking you back to your class for your dear Miss Fisher to see what she has done."

Aunty mumbled on as we walked up Tyne Street, crossed Hanover Street and continued up Tennant. I never looked up from the pavement. When we turned the corner at William Street, I started to drag my feet.

"I'm going to be sick, Aunty," I whimpered.

"You can be sick all that you want to, but after I have stated my business to your teacher. Now, young lady, you must move yourself. And as for being sick, don't worry, I'll take care of you should you boil over."

We stepped through the school gate and still I was wondering what her intentions could be. Was she going to take me to the principal's office? Was she going to cause a scandal? Oh, how I wished that this day never happened. As we entered the building, she asked me where my class was. I hesitated.

"You better tell me now or else I'll make even bigger trouble."

I had no choice but to show her the way. When we reached my classroom, she did not knock, she just pushed open the door, dragging me in behind her.

I could die from embarrassment and fear. I was shaking all over. I really felt like vomiting.

Aunty marched me up to Miss Fisher and asked me, "Is this the teacher that beat you so?"

I could just nod my head.

Aunty stepped up to the desk and took Miss Fisher's ruler. "Is this the ruler you used on the child? Why did you hit her?" she demanded.

30

"Because she was not listening in class. She's forever day-dreaming and I must make an example of her so that the children can have respect and obey me."

Aunty's eyes narrowed. "If you want the children's respect, you're not going to get it by beating them like this." And suddenly Aunty grabbed Miss Fisher's right hand and beat her with the wooden ruler in the same way as she had done to me.

Everything happened so fast, the children in the class did not even have a chance to scream as they would normally have done. They were too shocked at what they were witnessing. I was as good as paralysed with fear and this time I wished that I could just die right there in the classroom.

"Now listen to me carefully, Miss Fisher. This is the last time in your school career that you will do anything like this again. I promise you here and now, my dear teacher, that you have just received a little taste of your own medicine. And I'm sure it was not pleasant. Don't for one moment think that just because we live in District Six this gives you the right to treat the children so badly. You have much to learn and if you wish to make a court case about this, I will only be too willing to oblige because if you do, I'm taking Penny here," and she tapped me on my head with her finger, "immediately to our family doctor. And then I'm going down to Caledon Square to lay a charge of child abuse."

Miss Fisher apparently just stared at Aunty. I was too ashamed to look up at her, I just listened with my head hanging on my chest. I could hear my own heart beat.

To my amazement Miss Fisher whispered that she was sorry and that she did not know why she had reacted in the way that she had towards me.

"Not as long as I'm a teacher will I ever do something like this to any of my pupils," she stammered. "It's my first year of teaching and I'm scared of teaching in District Six. I've heard many stories about this place and they're not always nice. I'm a stranger here, I come from up country and board with a family in Walmer Estate. I have no intention of making a case. Can I take Penny to the first aid room and see to her hand?"

The other children told me that a slight smile crossed my aunty's face, and without a word she left me with the teacher. Miss Fisher asked the children to be quiet while we were gone, and told them to read. If they promised to be good, she would reward the whole class when we got back.

I was still holding my head down when she said, "Penny, lift up your head. This is not your fault and in future we will all work together, okay?"

I barely managed to whisper, "Yes, Miss, it's okay."

In the first aid room she washed my hand, soaked it in a solution that burned like fire, rubbed on some ointment and then bandaged it up. She soaked her own hand too and rubbed on the same ointment. But she did not bandage it up.

"It will draw too much attention and I want to keep this business as quiet as possible," she explained to me on the way back to the class.

We could not believe our eyes. All the children were sitting still, reading or pretending to read. I thought to myself: an angel must have descended on this lot because never in creation could a teacher get the children to sit still while she left the class.

Then we were in for another surprise. Miss Fisher reached for her bag and took out her purse and asked two of the bigger boys to go across to the shop in Tennant Street and buy twenty-six frozen suckers. The boys were out the door in a flash.

Then she said to me, "Penny, go and fetch your books and come and sit here in front in this open space where I can keep an eye on you."

I went to fetch my things. Before I was properly seated in my new bench, the boys were back. Miss Fisher handed each of us a frozen sucker as a reward for being so good. She told us to put our books away and then told us about herself: she came from Tulbagh where her father worked for the Forestry Department and they lived in a house in the pine forest. She was the youngest of five children and the only one who had the chance to study.

After this incident there was a better understanding between Miss Fisher and us. At the end of that year, I came second in her class and I received a book with the following inscription:

> To Penny, with love and best wishes.
> Always keep your head up high.
>
> *From your teacher Miss Fisher*

9 Inspection for lice and other things

SOME OF THE LADY TEACHERS at our primary school in William Street were really insensitive. Ever so often they ordered all the girls to line up in front of the class. The teacher then took two lead pencils to inspect our hair for lice. She made little "paths" in the hair and looked closely to see if there were any insects. If she discovered any, the child was commanded to stand in a corner of the room while she continued her inspection. The group in the corner usually grew to about twelve children. Some of them would be sent home immediately with a letter to tell their parents to clean their child's hair and inform them that the child could come back to school once the lice were gone.

Other children with heavily infested hair were sent to the Aspeling Street clinic to have their hair washed with a special solution that would kill off the lice and nits. But the worst happened one Monday morning when the Standard One teacher decided to made an example of a little girl whose head was always infested. So this time she marched the child out into the playground.

"Stand still," she hissed. "I've had enough of the dreaded lice and your filthy hair." And with that she took the pair of scissors she had brought from the classroom and grabbed hold of the girl's long tresses.

"But Miss, Mommy'll give me a hiding if I come home with my hair cut! And, Miss, it's not my fault that my hair is dirty! I try to keep my hair clean, but I can't help it if the lice keeps coming back. Please, Miss, don't!" the little girl pleaded.

But the teacher would not give in. "Whenever I go to your house to see your mother, then either she is not at home or she is drunk. I'm sorry," she said, "but it is for your own good that I'm cutting your hair."

She snipped and snipped until the little girl looked like a golliwog. Mercilessly the teacher marched the crying girl to the tap, told her to bend down and took a piece of soap from her pocket. She started to wash her hair under the cold water. The child screamed, broke loose and ran away.

A few minutes later the girl's mother walked into the school grounds, holding her daughter's hand. Luckily the mother was dressed decently this time and she had not yet had a drink. But she screamed and shouted and caused such a commotion that all the teachers left their classrooms to see what was happening. The noise was terrible and the mother's language atrocious. Within seconds all the children were outside in the school grounds.

The mother was uncontrollable. One male teacher tried to tell everyone to get back to their classrooms, but it was no use. People rushed in from the street to see what was going on. The crowd grew and grew, and so did the noise. The mother performed. She waved her arms and shook her finger in the teacher's direction while one of the male teachers tried to calm her down. He couldn't. She screamed that she was going to smash up the school, and that she was going to get even with the teacher who had done that to her little girl. In fact, she was going to get a gang together and bring them to the school.

"You were never at home when I went there to tell you about your daughter's hair, and when you were at home, you were too drunk for me to talk to you!" the teacher screamed back at her above the noise of the crowd.

"That's my business and so is my daughter, and you, you ugly bitch, just because you're educated and you got work as a teacher, that doesn't give you the right to mess up my little girl's hair? Drunk or not, she's my child and I love her. Do you have children? No, I can see you can't even have a man of your own, you're too damn ugly, and look at your hair! If it wasn't for these people holding me, you'd be black and blue before I'd finish you off!" the mother shrieked. "Your days are numbered, madam teacher, because when this child's father comes back from sea, he'll fix you and your kind up good and solid. Those guys that work on the boats are tough and rough and stand together, so be warned, dear madam teacher!"

By now the shouting could be heard in Tennant, William and Caledon Streets. More people gathered in the school grounds, and when they heard what had happened, they also joined in and went to the defence of the little girl and her mother.

"Where's that teacher? Bring her to me! See here, I have my knife with me, bring the bitch here so that I can rip her hair off with it. It's not very sharp but all of us can take a turn with a piece of it. Maybe that'll teach the bitch a lesson, because here in District Six we stand together. Others mustn't come and mess with our children," one scruffy-looking drunk old man shouted.

Then I overheard one of the mothers saying to another lady, "You know it's very wrong for the teacher to cut that child's hair, and let me tell you further, it's not just because of the lice and nits, a person can always get rid of them, but that teacher was always jealous of that child's beautiful hair."

"How do you know that the teacher was jealous?" the other woman asked.

"My daughter just told me so. She and that little girl are in the same class. Her name is Nancy. My daughter says that Nancy's hair was the longest and straightest in the class. And as you can see, that teacher has a kroes kop. But never mind, Nancy's hair will grow back again but the teacher's hair will always stay kinky."

The principal eventually managed to get a word in and he took Nancy and her mother to his office. The other male teachers got the pupils and teachers back into their classes, and the crowd unwillingly started to disperse. When everyone had left, the school gate was locked by the caretaker.

In District Six a secret was never a secret for long. It was later said that the principal must have used some kind of magic on Nancy's mother, because it was not very long before she left the school peacefully and with her mouth firmly shut.

Nancy was moved to another teacher's class and after that terrible episode an investigation was done into the procedure followed by teachers when they inspected the girls' hair. From then on, lice inspections were carried out by the school nurses who came around regularly. If there was anything wrong with a child, then the nurse would give him or her a letter to hand to the parents, and the matter would be handled from there on.

36

Fortunately for the teacher and the school, Nancy's mother did not carry out any of her threats. It was later said that she got the shock of her life when the principal spoke to her. She even settled down for the better. She did not drink as much as before, and often she was now waiting for Nancy outside the school gates. The two of them were sometimes seen walking hand in hand to Hanover Buildings in Hanover Street, where they occupied an upstairs room. Nancy's hair had started to grow again, although she actually looked quite pretty with short hair.

In that same school on the corner of Tennant and William Streets we had another kind of inspection. We had a male teacher in my Standard Two class who got the idea into his head to see if his pupils' necks were clean. At the same time he also checked their ears and nails for dirt. He inspected both girls and boys.

Then he went a bit further and decided that he was going to check the class's chests as well. First he would inspect the boys and then the girls. He told the girls to open the top buttons of their school shirts so that he could do his inspection to see if they were clean.

Clean indeed! He looked down their shirts to peep at their breasts! Luckily, most of the girls in the class were still undeveloped and flat-chested, but he had a good time looking at the girls who were not. In the beginning they were too naive and innocent to realise what his motive was and did as they were told. All except one, Judy, the only girl to wear a bra already.

When it was her turn Judy refused to open her shirt. She said she was clean and that he could see that she was always clean and tidy, every day, and that she could not understand why he wanted to look down her chest.

The teacher looked a bit embarrassed at her outburst and told one of the children to call the oldest lady teacher in the school.

When old Mrs Johnson arrived, he said something to her and told Judy to go with her. Up to this day we do not know whether or not Mrs Johnson inspected her, but Judy came back to the class with Mrs Johnson, who went up to the teacher and whispered something to him. It was not a very long conversation.

After this, our teacher never again dared to look down girls' shirts, because now the whole school knew about his strange method of inspection. Most of all the girls.

10 Navy blue bloomers

ALL THROUGH PRIMARY SCHOOL, navy blue bloomers were very much part of our school uniform. They were practical, strong and made from thick interlock material. But the girls did not like them. To tease them the boys even made up a jingle and would sometimes sing it when a girl passed them:

> There goes Aunty Soomers,
> In her navy bloomers.

All the girls hated this line!

The Little Wonder Store in Hanover Street always had these bloomers displayed in their shop window with a big price tag. It read "1/11d per pair". Amazingly enough the price of these bloomers never increased for as long as I was in primary school. It stayed one shilling eleven pennies. Even later when pounds,

J H Greshoff

George Hallett

Previous page: People lived upstairs and business was conducted downstairs in buildings that once displayed marvellous construction but which with time had become dilapidated - due to absentee landlords who were more interested in receiving rent than in maintaining their properties.

Above: It was obvious to everyone that 118 Hanover Street sold roti, curry and samosas. However, only customers knew about the dhaltjies, another Malay delicacy for which the Westminster was famous. And about the take-aways. On Friday evenings especially, mothers in the District would send their children with an emptly bowl to buy 2/6d worth of bean curry. This was eaten with fresh white bread dipped in the thick, spicy sauce.

J H Greshoff

One of the many barber shops dotted all over the District, where men gathered to enjoy a haircut, a shave and a chat. Sometimes a barber shop doubled up as a hairdressing saloon, like here, where Navsari no doubt would have heard the latest gossip from the ladies who came to have their hair straightened or curled – or both.

Noor Ebrahim

Colin de Vos

Above: The Western Building, constructed in 1930 on the corner of Longmarket, Upper Darling and Tennant Streets, housed a fish shop downstairs. Aunty Asa, the owner, saved many a poor child from going hungry by giving him or her steaming hot fish and chips.

Hadjie, who today has a stall on the Grand Parade in the centre of Cape Town, would have started out, like most hawkers did, with a hand-cart, then through hard work, progressed to a horse and cart, and finally to a bakkie. Here Hadjie is seen selling fruit and vegetables in Caledon Street some time in the seventies.

shillings and pence changed to Rands and cents, the price of the bloomers just changed to nineteen cents.

When we did physical training, the boys and girls were separated. The girls used the school playgrounds, a tarred quad facing William Street. The boys were taken to their own playground next to Caledon Street. This had a gravel surface and it was not pleasant to train there. So sometimes the girls and boys shared the school playground, but always using opposite sides.

One day the boys' instructor again decided that they should do their training in the quad. In our corner our teacher told us to take off our ties, gyms, shoes and socks. We normally did our exercises in our navy bloomers and white shirts. Not many girls had white PT dresses and white takkies, but those who did could wear them.

This particular Friday morning there were eight of us girls who were not wearing our bloomers. When the other girls started to undress, we gathered near the teacher. She noticed and asked, "Now what's the problem with you girls, why aren't you undressed yet?"

The bravest girl, Susan, said, "Miss, we are sorry but we all forgot to wear our navy bloomers, and some of us are wearing nylon panties which are thin, Miss. Also Miss, the boys on the other side of the playground will look at us, Miss, and Miss could you please excuse us for today and we all promise that in the future we'll never forget to wear our navy blue bloomers."

"Never forget! I have heard this story before and all I can say is that the lot of you want to show me that you want to be old before your time. Well, little madams, I have news for you. If that is what your intentions are, then today is the day that you're going to be taught a very good lesson."

She leaned on the cane she used to keep us in line with.

"I have given in to your excuses in the past, and what happens? You show me here on this day that you do not take me seriously.

But now, my dear young ladies, your time has run out. I already discussed your convenient forgetfulness on PT days with the principal last time, and he instructed me to bring those who do not wish to adhere to the school rules to his office so that he can see for himself and do the necessary. He's well aware that I have spoken and given out warnings more than once that you should be dressed according to school regulations." She was completely out of breath after such a long speech.

"Please, Miss," Susan insisted, "we'll do anything, just don't make us get undressed. We will stay after school, we'll clean the classroom, we'll even scrub the floor. But please, we beg you, don't let us undress."

Miss Roberts stared at Susan and whisked her long cane through the air. It made us jump. Then she said very calmly, "Now! I want you lot to take off your ties and gyms immediately and follow me, and no talking. And you other lot," she addressed the others, "go on and make up a netball team and start playing. And remember to behave yourselves. I'll be back in a few minutes."

We had no choice. With glowing faces we pulled our gyms over our heads and off Miss Roberts marched us to the principal's office. As we walked along we tried to hide behind each other.

"Walk in single file!" Miss Roberts said. We did, but trying all the time to pull our shirts down so that they could cover our panties. It did not help much.

That march to the principal's office was taking an eternity, and we still had to pass the boys who were were practising gymnastics next to the school buildings. Some boys were doing somersaults. One landed on the tar instead of on the mat because he lost his concentration trying to look at us.

"There goes all the Aunty Soomers without their navy bloomers!" shouted another. Their teacher told the boys to be quiet and behave, but we could see that he was just as amused as they were.

When we reached the principal's office he was not there. "Stand up straight against the wall and wait right here," Miss Roberts said and disappeared to fetch him. We all wondered what Mr Hendricks was going to do with us. He was such a nice man.

Within seconds the two were back. "Thank you, Miss Roberts, you can go back to the other girls now. I'll take care of these." Mr Hendricks had a funny grin on his face when he looked at us. We all hung our heads.

"Stand up straight!"

We all jumped.

"I know everyone of you. I know your parents and I know the homes you come from. I know that you all have your proper uniforms and that you're just being defiant, thinking you're big now and needn't wear what the other girls wear. And you, Susan," he said, looking her straight in the eye, "always the bold speaker, where is your tongue now? Oh, I see that you choose not to speak. Just as well. I want to inform you, Susan, that I have spoken to your father before, because this is, as you know, not the first time that you have refused to wear your proper school uniform. Your father said that I must do what I think is best if you disobey school rules again."

We had no idea that he knew Susan's father was a very rich businessman and they lived in Walmer Estate. In fact, we all wanted to be like Susan. She always had the best of everything. Her lunch was wrapped in a pure white starched napkin, and sometimes she even brought cold chicken to school. Most Decembers her dad took their whole family to Johannesburg by plane for a holiday. And she never seemed to be afraid to speak. She always looked so confident. But now she did not say a word.

"Stand up straight, your backs against the wall," Mr Hendricks ordered. "Now, stretch your arms above your heads."

We did as we were told, and while doing so our blouses pulled up and our nylon panties showed.

We nearly died of embarrassment.

"Now turn around, faces to the wall and touch your toes."

When we had our backsides in the air, he whisked his cane across all of our buttocks in one quick motion. It was not painful as he did not strike us hard, but the thought of it was terrible.

"Now, can you see how important it is for you girls to wear your navy blue bloomers? It is nice and protective. Go back to your teacher and you, Susan, tell her that I told you that you can all get dressed."

It turned out that Susan's dad and our principal attended the same high school when they were young.

11   Picking a fight

THERE WAS A GIRL in Standard Five who disliked me. We were in the same standard but in different classes. Farieda was in the same class as my best friend Jane. She was older than us and more developed as she had failed two of her previous standards.

Farieda and I had never quarrelled, but for some reason she couldn't stand me. Although she came from a respected Muslim family she was a bit on the wild side and I didn't like the company that she was keeping. To my mind she was not my type, but I never told anybody this because if she ever found out, my life at school would have been turned into a real hell.

Farieda considered herself to be a "main guy". She would

throw her own books down on the pavement, on purpose, and then force a meek child to pick them up and hand them to her. And if she ordered someone to do something for her, they had to do it, otherwise they would be in trouble.

Farieda tried to force Jane, my best friend, to be her friend. Jane confessed to me that she didn't like Farieda, but didn't know how to tell her that she wanted nothing to do with her and her friends, so she just tried to stay out of her way.

One day during our long lunch break, Farieda saw a reason to pick a fight with me. That morning my mother had given me one of my brother Ron's old shirts to wear. I liked the shirt because it was made of a nice soft material. It was a creamy white colour and had a tiny loop to the side of the collar that tied around a small button. It was winter and I wore a tie and my school jersey over the shirt. I was happy the way I was dressed, and in any case, my own shirts were all still wet. It had been raining for a few days and the washing wouldn't dry.

Farieda walked up to me and in front of all the other children out in the school grounds shouted, "Look everybody, Penny's wearing her brother's shirt!"

Everyone laughed at me and some children made nasty remarks. I looked at Farieda and said, "So what, why don't you mind your own business and leave me alone? My mother gave me this shirt to wear and I happen to like it. It's too small for my brother. Besides, it's been paid for and it's clean."

She glared at me.

I suggested, "Maybe you're jealous? Do you know that this shirt is high fashion? See this little loop? It's pretty, isn't it? I'm sure you've never had a shirt like this. But if you like it you can have it," I added, just to make her angry.

Farieda jumped up and attacked me. She ripped at the top of the shirt so that the button snapped off.

Then I got mad. I wasn't prepared to be beaten up by Farieda. I was very scared of her and I was even more frightened of the possibility of anybody telling my father that I was seen fighting. I knew that he would not approve of his daughter fighting in the street or at school. But, I thought, if he should find out I'll handle that punishment later.

So I grabbed at Farieda's shoulders and she pulled my hair. I let go and pulled her hair. She screamed. We continued attacking each other, she scratching my cheeks and I smacking her in the face. By now a crowd was beginning to form around us and I did not want one of the teachers to catch me fighting, so I ran to the girls' toilets at the back of the school where I knew she would follow me. Farieda came after me at full speed.

Running just a few steps ahead of her, I was thinking that lunch break was almost over and I still had to comb my hair and pull my clothes straight. My heart was pounding. I was nervous and confused. I thought that we should rather stop the fight, but I didn't want Farieda to win and then be in a position to boss me around. On the other hand, I didn't want my parents or teachers to know about the fighting. Terrible thoughts flashed through my mind. The principal would punish me, he could even expel me. And my father had warned us that if we, his children, should ever bring shame on the family, then we'd be sent away to a home for delinquent children. I was never sure if he meant what he said, but I was not prepared to take the risk.

As I dashed into the girls' toilets I was still undecided. I chose the first door and to my horror this toilet was all blocked up, filthy and smelly. When I turned round Farieda was standing right in front of me. In desperation I jumped on top of the brick ledge on either side of the flush toilet.

The smell was unbearable. I had one foot placed on either side of the pot. I felt nauseous. This is the end of me, I thought. Just then Farieda jumped up towards me, and as she did, I jumped down. She tried to grab hold of me but her foot slipped and she landed in the slops!

I made my escape and outside, I straightened myself out. Jane came to my assistance and gave me her comb. I ran it through my hair and she helped me tie my ribbon. My shirt had been torn, but I tied my jersey buttons right to the top so that you wouldn't notice.

I was still shaking with nervousness, but being almost myself again, I told the other girls about Farieda's mishap. They all burst out laughing, all except some of her chums who said I better watch out because she would definitely come after me soon. I didn't want to think about the future just then. Fortunately the bell rang and we had to go back to our classes.

Farieda did not come out of the toilets.

Some time that afternoon I heard that she had waited for all the children to go back to their classes before she sneaked home. They lived right next to the school and she got herself cleaned up there before she came back to her class, making some excuse for being late. And then, just before the last period, I received a message from one of the girls in Farieda's class that there was going to be a fight after school. This was to take place on the boys' playground and I was ordered to be there!

I was worried. What if she beat me up? What if she'd brought back a knife from home with her? What if I landed in hospital? I could even lose my life and what about the shame that I would bring on our family and the school?

I decided the best way out was the coward's way, and that was to run home. I had to be out of my class as soon as the bell rang. I had no time to waste as my life was at stake here.

The moment the bell rang, I rushed out of the class and ran down Tennant Street as fast as my legs could carry me. But running did not help. Farieda's chums caught up with me on the corner of Hanover and Tennant Streets. Out in the street I did not want to draw attention to myself because if anyone saw me they would fetch my mother straight away. Besides, I would be labelled a sissy for first running away and then having my mother come to save me.

But I didn't really have a choice. One of Farieda's chums wrestled my case from me, while the others formed a circle around me and practically dragged me back to the school. I was so embarrassed and shaky that I could hardly walk. My only support was Jane, who shyly followed behind. When we reached the school grounds, all the teachers had already left. I was marched to the boys' gravel playground. I hated the gravel stones because once I had fallen there and got my hands and knees badly scraped. Whatever else happens, I thought, I have to avoid falling at all cost.

Immediately one of Farieda's friends attacked me. I scratched her and ripped her dress. She had not expected me to defend myself so viciously. She leapt away from me and shouted at Farieda, "Now see what I look like! What am I supposed to tell my mother when I get home? I can't fix this dress. I tell you, I won't be hanging out with you any more. You're nothing but trouble!"

"That's okay with me, you sissy," Farieda sneered back. "I still have my other friends."

The ex-friend answered, "Friends indeed, but I wonder for how long." And then she left to go and face her mother at home.

Then my Number One enemy reached for me. As she dashed towards me I jumped out of the way. It took her by surprise and she fell flat on her face on the gravel stones. I knew that she was hurt because before the fight she had removed her school blazer and rolled up her shirt sleeves.

46

Farieda looked dazed. Her elbows were scraped and her one knee was bleeding. Suddenly I felt sorry for her and I wanted to help her up but Jane whispered in my ear, "Run, Penny, get away before all her chums attack you!"

I hesitated but Jane picked up her school case and mine in one hand, grabbed me by the arm with the other and away we were. We flew down Tennant Street and only when we reached the corner of Godfrey and Hanover Streets did we stop to check if we were being followed.

There was no-one behind us so we stopped for a breather.

"You know, Penny, I never knew you could fight like that," Jane panted.

"But I can't. If my father gets to hear about this, I might as well go and pack my things."

"Your father will never send you away," Jane said. "He only says so, I'm sure he'll say you'd be a fool if you didn't defend yourself. Remember he was a soldier."

I hadn't thought of that, so I said, "As for me being a fighter, I think luck was on my side. It could have been me who fell into that stinking toilet pot, you know." And we both laughed till our sides ached.

I didn't tell my mother anything and quickly fixed my torn shirt while she was sitting outside in the sun. But I could not wait for my brother Ron to get home. I had to speak to him as soon as possible. I needed help and I knew that I could trust him. He had already received his black belt in judo.

Ron and my father eventually arrived home together from their work place in Roeland Street. Only after supper did I get a chance to talk to him alone. I first made him swear not to tell our parents. He agreed, and I told him everything. When I said who the girl was, he said he knew her because he was friends with her brother and they attended the same judo classes.

"Now leave everything in my hands," Ron said. "I'm going to ask Dad if you can take judo lessons with me."

"Do you think Dad will allow me to?"

"Of course he'll let you come. You'll be with me."

Ron went to my parents' room where he discussed my judo lessons. My dad agreed and said that it was good that I should learn to protect myself, especially here in District Six. You never knew when you might need it. Then he cautioned me, "Now, Penny, don't broadcast or brag about your judo lessons. Some people might challenge you to a fight to see if you're any good."

Dear Dad, I thought to myself, if only you knew what your daughter has been through today!

The following day I went to school full of confidence, and Farieda stayed out of my way. I also avoided her. I had no wish for more trouble. But before the end of the day Jane came to tell me Farieda hadn't given up. She was planning another fight for later. This did not bother me because I knew her brother was in the same judo class as Ron, and I could not wait for the time to arrive for my first judo lesson.

I had a very light supper while the sun was still high. By the time Ron came home from work, I was all ready and set to go for my first lesson.

"Not so fast! Classes start at seven thirty, and it's only six o'clock!" he said. He took a bath but he did not eat.

"Why don't you eat?" I asked.

"Because you can't do exercise on a full stomach. Have you eaten?" he asked.

"Only very little and much earlier on," I said.

When we eventually arrived at the gym upstairs at St Mark's Preparatory School in William Street, I was all excited. The guys rolled out a large foam mat, which was covered in thick, royal blue leatherette material. Ron introduced me to the members of the club and then I met Farieda's brother Bienjamin. He looked like a nice person, not a bit like his mean sister.

"Are you Farieda's brother?" I asked, and he said yes, and so I said, "You must tell your sister that you met me and that I've now also joined the judo club."

"It'll be a pleasure to mention you to her," he promised.

Taking judo classes was not as easy as I thought it would be. We had to do warm-up exercises for about fifteen minutes. Then we were told to sit on the mat while two members demonstrated. We were then formed into groups according to the grades. As I was a newcomer I had to sit quietly and watch what went on until the instructor had time for me. He first explained many things about judo and told me that at the next class I would learn more, but in the meantime I should keep fit and study a book on judo that he gave me.

It was a great disappointment. I wanted to learn how to throw someone to the ground straight away, so that I could tackle Farieda when she picked another fight, but I realised my progress would be much too slow for that. And in fact, I never once used judo in a real fight.

Farieda was still rude towards me, but we both kept our distance. Maybe just knowing about the judo did the trick. We both passed our exams at the end of that year, and I went on to high school. Farieda had found herself a job at a clothing factory, and so she dropped out of school.

The last time I heard about her was when her brother mentioned at the judo club that she had got herself pregnant and was going to be married. Good for her, I thought, maybe being a wife and a mother will calm her down.

12   Learning to smoke

MANY OF THE PEOPLE in District Six smoked. Some smoked tobacco while others smoked dagga. Those who smoked tobacco smoked cigarettes. Those who smoked dagga smoked zolls or pipes made from the broken-off necks of glass bottles. Cigarettes could be bought at any shop while dagga was sold only by special dealers. It was supposed to be a secret that some people were "dagga merchants", but as there were no secrets in District Six everybody knew about them. Yet there were times that you pretended not to be aware of any such thing because you knew it was best to mind your own business. It was also well known that if you wished to buy dagga you had to know the specific slang that was spoken amongst the dagga merchants and smokers before you would be supplied.

Shirley and I thought that smoking cigarettes must be fun. People who smoked looked so good with a cigarette in their mouths, especially the posh ladies with long, red-painted nails who appeared very elegant holding a cigarette holder.

Shirley was seven and I was eight years old when we thought it was about time to find out about smoking. Some boys in our street who were younger than us had already acquired the habit. Our dad and Aunty also smoked, so it really couldn't be too bad. One morning we took a box of matches from the kitchen and went into the street. In our street there was hardly any place to hide, but it was a very windy day and luckily not many people were about. After carefully looking around, we decided to try our experiment on the stoep of the neighbour across the road from us. There was a bit of a wall behind which we could hide. So, armed with a newspaper and our box of matches, we got started.

I took a piece of paper and rolled it up the way the vagrants did when they had no cigarettes to smoke. Just like them, we lit our rolled newspaper cigarettes and puffed away on the burning paper. The wind blew the smoke into our faces and we got scared. What if we were to burn our fingers, our lips, eyebrows or hair? We decided that this was a bit too dangerous. Smoking a newspaper zoll was no fun at all. What we needed was real cigarettes. I happened to have a tickey in my dress pocket and I told Shirley to wait for me on the stoep while I went to Kader's shop to buy two Cavella cigarettes. I had no idea what it would cost because my dad never bought loose cigarettes – it was cheaper to buy them by the packet. I asked for two cigarettes and got a halfpenny change, with which I bought two loose sweets. I thought that after smoking, a sweet would be just the right thing to take the smell of the smoke away.

Before I could slip out of the shop, the shopkeeper asked, "For who's those cigarettes?"

"For my aunty," I said, "and she said that I could buy sweets from the change."

He believed me and I placed the cigarettes together with the sweets in my dress pocket and hurried back to Shirley.

After many false starts we finally got the cigarettes to burn. We puffed and puffed. The smoke and the smell made us both choke and cough so much that tears were soon streaming from our eyes. Suddenly we got a huge shock. The front door had opened and there the lady of the house stood, looking at us.

"I heard a noise, but I never expected to see the two of you smoking on my stoep," she said with narrowed eyes.

We tried to hide the burning cigarettes behind our backs, but it was no use. We had been caught red-handed.

"This is surely a case for your parents to handle," Mrs Adams said.

We were too frightened to say anything and just stared at her with big, innocent eyes, full of tears from the smoke. But then we started pleading with her not to give us away.

"But why are you smoking?" she asked.

Neither of us could answer. We waited, agonising about what her decision would be. In a harsh voice she finally said, "Clean up this mess, and I want you both to swear to me that you will never, ever, smoke again. And don't just stand there, get moving with the cleaning up! Your father should know about this, your mother is too soft. She won't punish you enough. Yes, your father should be told. I'm sure that he'll beat your backsides till the skin comes off so that you will remember this day forever!"

It will be better if Shirley and I run away from home, I thought as we started to clean up the mess. But there was no chance to do so. Harshly Mrs Adams took the left-over cigarettes from us, crushed them in her hands and flung the whole lot into the street. By now, we both had the shakes and started to cry and sob, "We promise that we'll never, never, ever smoke again. Please just don't tell our father."

Mrs Adams didn't say anything. She just looked at us sternly. When she at last spoke, she said, "Go home now, you two, and go and wash your hands and faces. I won't tell your father, but I will surely tell your mother so that she can talk to you about the dangers of smoking at such a young age."

We stood if we were transfixed to the cement floor.

"Go on now, don't just stand there. And remember, I'll be watching the two of you in future."

Mrs Adams did speak to my mother, but only the following day after my father had left for work.

Ron was about thirteen when Dad found a packet of cigarettes in his pocket. Dad was so furious that he made Ron eat the cigarettes on the spot. It was horrible. Ron and I were very close and I was terribly upset. Mom was in the backyard and she had no idea of what was happening inside the house, so I hurried her into the house and I quickly told her. Dad was forcing another handful of cigarettes into Ron's mouth and she rushed to pull him away. Dad pushed her to one side, none too gently, and told her to leave him alone.

"Ron's getting too big for his own boots, he must be taught a lesson. If he wants to smoke this stuff then I'll make him eat it first!"

"Leave the child alone," Mom said. "Can't you see that he's had enough and that you're making him sick?"

In the background I was screaming and begging my father to stop. And then Ron vomited and got quite sick. When my father saw how sick Ron was getting he turned to go. Before he left the room, he turned to me, warning, "And you remember this day, too. If I should ever catch you smoking I'll treat you in the same way."

Thank goodness you never found out about Shirley and me smoking, I thought to myself – bless Mrs Adams for not telling you.

Mom took Ron to the kitchen and gave him milk to drink to make him feel better. She told him not to carry cigarettes on him while he was so young; his time would come for things like that.

Ron never said a word to her as he was still too shocked from the treatment he had received from Dad. He was exceptionally quiet all evening and would not eat his supper.

When we went to bed that night, he still hadn't said a thing. I tried to sleep but found it difficult. Everything that had happened came back into my mind over and over again. I was very fond of Ron and I was worried about him. In the end, I got out of bed and tiptoed to the lower end of the passage. Ron was not in his folding bed. (When Ron turned thirteen he decided that he needed privacy, so he moved his bed into the passage. Every morning he folded it away, pulled the fitted floral cover over it and stored it against the wall.)

I continued down the long passage to the front door. There I froze in my tracks. Ron had his mountaineering haversack on his back and he was pushing his bicycle very quietly down the passage! I ran to the front door, trying to make as little noise as possible, and placed my arms across it. Then it struck me that Ron had been so quiet all evening because he was making plans to run away. I started crying and begged him not to go.

"Dad will catch up with you wherever you go and then you will be punished even worse," I sobbed.

"I have to go because I'll never forget the way Dad treated me this afternoon. I do not wish to live in the same house as him. All my friends have started to smoke and I also wanted to try it. And anyway, Dad is very unfair because he also smokes."

"Well, it was stupid of you to forget the cigarettes in your pocket," I told him. But Ron took no notice of me and tried to get me away from the door so that he could leave.

"Listen, Ron," I threatened, "it's the middle of the night and if you leave, I'm going to shout. And when they discover that you planned to run away, you'll be punished all over again."

I would not leave the door and carried on talking softly. "Where are you going to go? We don't have any family except for Uncle Peter in Elsies River and you know as well as I that there will be no room for you with them."

After much persuasion, Ron decided to stay. Everyone in the house was still sleeping peacefully. He put his bike away and I quickly helped him unpack the haversack. Before he said good-night to me Ron said in a quiet voice, "If I should ever catch my children smoking one day, I'll never do what Dad did to me. I'd think of some better way to discourage them from smoking."

Ron kept his distance from Dad for many years. In the meanwhile the younger boys in the house had all discovered the art of smoking. Dad knew, but he did not have the energy to dish out punishment as he liberally as he used to do.

13 Lanes and rooftops, robbers and robberies

THE LANES AND ROOFTOPS of District Six were among the favourite hiding places for the many gangsters in the area and their stolen goods. Being a very adventurous and inquisitive child, I liked to go through our backyard door and into the service lane.

Our lane ran with an L-bend from Godfrey Street, first parallel to Roger Street and, after the bend, parallel to Tyne Street. The bit that ran along the back of our house, being number 14, and the neighbours' houses, numbers 12 and 10, could not be seen from the road. For this reason and because it didn't run through to Parkin Street but ended in a cul de sac behind our neighbours' backyard, it was an ideal hiding place, and often people who were being chased by the police or members of other gangs would end up hiding there.

One afternoon, my mother and I were alone at home when she told me that the drain in our backyard was blocked. The two of us went into the lane where the lid of the drain was, and together we lifted the heavy metal square.

It was immediately clear what had caused the blockage: we found a large sugar bag stashed away in the drain.

We looked at each other, then around us to see if anyone was watching us, and then we pulled the heavy bag from the hole. It was a bit of a struggle, but eventually we managed to untie the string. To our surprise the bag was filled with bottles of wine and a packet wrapped in plastic.

"Looks like dagga to me," my mother said. "We'd better close the bag up exactly the way we found it and replace the lid."

While we were busy she told me not to mention what we had seen in the drain. "Not a word," she said.

"Why?" I asked.

"We can get into trouble because people may think the bag belongs to us."

We left the lane and hoped that whoever the bag belonged to would remove it soon as it became dark.

I could hardly swallow my food at supper table that evening. I kept imagining that I heard someone moving in the lane.

Only at nine o'clock that night, the bag was removed. We knew because the water in the yard suddenly ran away smoothly.

Pete and Jimmy on the roof of Tyne Street number 14

56

I liked to escape from the noise inside the house onto our rooftop. We had a flat roof and I would climb up with the ladder that always stood in our backyard. From our rooftop we had the most beautiful view of Table Mountain, Devil's Peak, Lion's Head, central Cape Town and the docks.

It was a millionaire's view. Many times there were big ships docked in the harbour, or I stood and watched an ocean liner enter Table Bay harbour. Then a twenty-one gun salute would be fired from Signal Hill. From the rooftop one could see the smoke, and the volleys could be heard all over Cape Town.

Sometimes I was unaware of the time and got a big fright when the cannon was fired at midday. Only afterwards would I remember that it was the cannon on Signal Hill letting the people in the city know that it was twelve noon.

On one of my expeditions onto the roof I discovered a small bag of dagga cigarettes hidden in a crack in the wall. I had noticed that the paint had been scraped away and that one crack had been made bigger, so I investigated. I took one look and pushed the small bag back into the crack and scuttled down the ladder.

I didn't tell anybody because I was not supposed to be up on the roof, and I knew very well that things like that were better not talked about. But sometimes when the southeaster blew so fiercely in the night, one could hear all kinds of strange noises, even inside the house. Were there people in the lane, we would wonder, or maybe on the roof? And what were they hiding?

According to the newspapers and to outsiders, District Six was a notorious place. Visitors who had nasty surprises there warned others not to go near it. What they should have said was that Friday and Saturday nights were not very good times to be in this unfamiliar territory.

In fact, not only on weekend nights did strangers have to be careful, they needed to be on the lookout for thieves and robbers all of Saturday. The people of the District were aware of this, but most strangers were not.

People who grew up and lived in District Six knew everyone who belonged in the area. So did the gangsters, who grew up there and lived there. They recognised strangers immediately, and some of them would linger about, waiting to rob an unsuspecting victim. They never bothered any of us living in District Six.

It was a Saturday summer afternoon and the weather was beautiful. Not a breath of southeaster. Most of the people in our street were sitting outside enjoying the lovely sunshine. I'd just gone inside to fetch something, when I heard a loud commotion in the street.

"That's right, give that hooligan a jolly good hiding!" people were screaming.

"Yes!" Boeta Bruima shouted, "I got a aapstert at home, I think I'll go and fetch it." And he went to get his whip.

"Ag, shame," Aunty Sofie of Aspeling Street shouted after him, "leave him alone, man. Can't you see he's drunk and good for nutting?"

Outside Kika's shop Mrs Adams and Dora were standing smoking cigarettes.

Oh please, don't let there be another fight, I thought to myself. Then I noticed that everybody was crowded around my dad. I went closer. He was holding a drunken guy by the scruff of the neck. To one side a stranger, dressed in a suit, white shirt and tie, was looking on. Now nobody in District Six would be dressed like that on a Saturday afternoon! Saturday was a day for casual clothes; only on Sundays would the men wear a collar and tie to church.

58

"I know who you are, you live in the Mokkies Building, and I know your father," my dad was saying to the hooligan. "The two of us work together and he's always complaining to me about how bad you've turned out. He's told me that if he receives any more complaints about you he's going to make arrangements to have you sent away to a reform school."

Dad tightened his hold on the young man's neck. As the hooligan cringed and tried to pull away, Mrs Khan, a Muslim lady, shouted from her stoep, "Hey, Mr Alex, don't still talk nice to the rubbies. Here, give him to me so that I can beat him with my rolling pin!"

From across the street Mrs Adams shouted, "Hey, Khan, what you doing with a rolling pin in your hands? Is it your habit to be out on such a nice day with that thing in your hands?"

"Ag man, Adams, you know mos that I'm making rotis for that café in Caledon Street," Mrs Kahn said. "But this afternoon I feel like using my rolling pin on that lowlife's head. Don't you think that he got a damned cheek to come here into our area to rob that nice gentleman?"

"Hey, what's it with you, Kahn?" came the answer from across the street. "First you want to beat that skollie with your rolling pin, and now you saying nice things about a stranger. Seem to me that you on the lookout for a man, hey? But maybe it's about time too as your old man left you years ago. Must have been that sharp mouth of yours that drove him away."

Mrs Khan pointed the rolling pin at her, shouting, "If you don't shut your mouth I'll cause a scene and then we can have two fights in Tyne Street today."

Mrs Adams smiled and said, "Hey, Khan, you know that I'm only joking. But anyway, maybe one day you'll tell me why your old man left you."

59

All the while the stranger looked like he didn't understand what was happening. My dad had retrieved his possessions from the hooligan, who was begging him not to tell his father about how drunk he was and please not to mention that he had attacked and robbed the stranger.

My dad also took a knife from him which was sticking out of his back pocket. "Now make yourself scarce and never attempt to do to anybody what you did in our street today or I'll take you personally to the Charge Office in Caledon Street," he told him none too gently. "What is it again that they call you, Michael?" he added. "I know you got a nickname."

"Bones," the hooligan said, "everybody calls me Bones because I'm so thin." Then Bones went over to the stranger, told him that he was very sorry and walked away, looking like a dog with his tail between his legs.

Someone in the crowd called after him, "Old Bones' face won't be seen around here for a long time, and let's hope the poor thing has learnt a lesson here today."

There was laughter all around.

Mrs Khan, who had still not returned to her roti making, shouted, "Hey, Mr Alex, you people are too soft with the skollies. Do you know what they do with people like that in Mecca?"

"Yes, Mrs Khan, I know what they do to them because remember? I spent a few years in Cairo and El Alamein when I was in the army, but this is District Six and here life is different!"

My dad had given the wallet back to the stranger. The poor man was now looking for his hat which had fallen off in the scuffle. Suddenly Mrs Khan grabbed a scruffy little boy by the neck and took the hat from him. "Want to steal the nice gentleman's hat, hey!" she cried.

"Is not true, I picked it up to give it back to the uncle."

60

Mrs Kahn pulled his ear and said to him, "You dirty little liar, I could see you were going to run away with it!" She shoved him about a bit and shouted, "You little loafer, you don't belong here in this street, go on, get going and don't ever let me see you around here again. I promise you that I know a policeman and I'll ask him to give you a beating with his sjambok."

My mother had taken the stranger into our house so that he could tidy himself. She offered him tea, but he refused just as my dad entered. So Dad said to me, "Penny, go and fetch two glasses and my bottle of Old Brown Sherry."

I did as I was asked and I went to sit next to my mother.

"This is Mr Jonathan Damons," my dad introduced the stranger. "He lives in Bridgetown."

Mom apologised to Mr Damons for the treatment he had received in District Six. She told him that it was very seldom that we had trouble in our street as everybody living here was decent. It was mostly people from other areas that came looking for trouble here. (My mother didn't mention anything about "The Building" lower down in our street!)

Mr Jonathan Damons had an aunt in Aspeling Street; in fact, he had just come from her when he was attacked. He used to come to District Six at least once a month to visit his relative. After that episode he was never bothered by hooligans again. Sometimes he would come round to our house and bring sweets for us children, and once he brought flowers from his garden in Bridgetown.

My dad was respected by the gangsters, and whenever we children were out on the street and the gangsters wanted to interfere with us, one of the gang members would know us.

"Hey, leave that gentleman's children alone," he'd say.

They knew that my dad would not take any nonsense from them. If they knew you weren't scared of them, they respected you.

But the gangsters robbed and stole from the Jewish shops and there was always big drama. The people of District Six called it "free entertainment". Especially if they picked Shrand's shoe shop. This smart shop on the corner of Hanover and Tyne Streets was broken into many times, even in broad daylight. The alarm system would go off, people would run in all directions, the Law would come. But by the time the police arrived, the thieves would already have gone off, loaded with their stolen goods.

These were experienced thieves. In the commotion that followed a theft, some of them would pretend that they, too, were looking for the culprits. No bystander ever told the truth and no one ever saw or knew anything when questioned by policemen. If the Law asked which direction the thieves had gone, someone would always point the opposite way. Later in the week you would see children and grown-ups wearing brand new shoes that were obviously stolen. They would even dare to walk right past Shrand's shoe shop and stop to do window shopping!

14 Shops

ALL THE SHOPS IN DISTRICT SIX did a roaring trade. Most of the big shops were in Hanover Street. There was the famous Maxim's, Mr Goodman's shop in the Sweeteries Building, which sold the best peanuts in town. And for sixpence you got a bag of sweets that could last you a few days.

Mr Johnson's shop, facing Tyne Street, sold a little of everything. We children had a standing order for certain comic books and magazines – School Friend and June magazine for the girls, and Sad Sack, Beano, The Dandy and Valiant comics for the boys. Your order had to be placed in advance, otherwise you had to go down to the CNA in Plein Street in town.

Waynik's were famous for their school uniforms. When they opened, a new era started for us. In the beginning, all the girls in primary school wore the same school uniform all the year round – a gym, a white blouse, a tie, a girdle and a school hat. And of course the navy blue bloomers! When it was cold, we added a navy blue jersey or a blazer. But when Waynik's introduced new school uniforms in different fabrics and designs, things started to change. We now had to get a summer uniform as well. The summer school dress could be bought ready-made, or otherwise the material was bought from the shop and your mother had the dress made at one of the many dressmakers in the District.

Just before the schools reopened for a new year, Waynik's shop was packed with customers. They arrived from all over to buy school uniforms. The children had to come along with their mothers so that they could fit on their new uniforms. Sometimes you could hardly get into the shop, it was so full, and you had to wait very long before you got served. But you didn't mind, because it was always exciting going to school in a new uniform. If you got a new pair of shoes as well, you'd walk around with a smile on your face, a spring in your step, and ever so often glance down to see just how good the shoes looked on your feet!

There were many shoe shops in Hanover Street. Manta's shoe shop was one of the largest. Then there was this one old Jewish shoe shop close to the Star bioscope whose owner never changed his shoe display in the window. Year in and year out the same old styles stayed in the window. With time, some of the leather faded in colour, but nothing else ever changed.

And we of course had our own famous shoe shop in Tyne Street: Shrand's. It was very different from the old Jew's shop – the shop windows were at all times professionally arranged with the prices neatly displayed on the shoes.

The prices were too expensive for our family. Early on, when we were only three children in the house, my mother bought our Christmas shoes from Shrand's. They were Jack and Jills, and on opening the shoe boxes Ron and Shirley and I would always find a balloon inside. Later, when we were eight children, my mother could no longer afford to buy from Shrand's, so our shoes were bought from Edworks down in Plein Street where the shoes were cheaper than anywhere in the District.

Janjira's, who sold groceries, was one of the busiest shops in Hanover Street, and the cheapest too. This shop was always packed with customers. On Friday late afternoons it was filled from the counter to the door with people asking for sugar and Cerebos salt, Five Roses or Joko tea, Gold Cross or Nestlé condensed milk, Southall's coffee, Cartwright's curry powder, long-grain white rice, sugar beans, grease-proof paper, bottles of vinegar, Snowflake cake flour, mieliemeel and Jungle oats.

At Banks Hiring Supply you could sort out chipped cups that were displayed in a big enamel bath on the pavement outside the shop. If you looked carefully you could find multi-coloured cups with hardly any chips on them, costing five pence each. There were saucers available too, and these cost half the price of the cups.

But the "Rooikop Jood" was our favourite shop. The tall, good-looking shopkeeper with his fiery head of hair and his assistants knew all their customers by name. They knew all the children's parents. They also knew what brand of item to give to which child, as some families bought only certain brands of food.

The Rooikop Jood was a wizard at adding up. Even when they were later used all over the place, he never got a calculator. On the counter there were always large sheets of brown or white paper. He would tear off a piece and scribble your prices down and add them up in no time. He never made a mistake. After you paid for your goods he would hand you your change together with the slip. Once home, we would first check our items and then do our own addition. It would take a lot longer, and eventually we would always be satisfied that the Rooikop Jood was right.

The Rooikop Jood was also famous for his snoekmootjies – thick pieces of raw snoek, folded double, that were preserved in a large wooden barrel filled with vinegar and spices. My mother often bought snoekmootjies which she steamed slightly and served with butter and bread. Sometimes the steamed snoek was flaked and braised with onions, fish oil, tomatoes, small pieces of potatoes and chillies. Smoorsnoek was usually eaten with white long-grain rice or bread and butter. One could also buy the normal dry, salted snoek from the Rooikop Jood. His fish oil – cooking oil – wasn't sold in sealed bottles. You had to bring your own bottle and this he or an assistant would fill, or half fill, by pumping oil from a big drum at the back of the store.

There were also many vegetable and fruit shops, butcheries that catered for the Christians, and Muslim butcheries that sold strictly halaal meat. The dairy next to Voetberg's shop in Hanover Street, opposite the Rose & Crown bar, sold the freshest full-cream milk, butter, cheese and lovely cakes. Auntie Lettie's speciality was a twisted egg loaf – the Jewish people call this a kitke – and rye bread. My mother used to buy one of each of these on a Saturday morning.

Hanover Street also had its own herbalist shop close to Castle Bridge, and its own barbers and hairdressers, drapery and clothes shops.

But the famous Van der Schyff's dress material shop was on the corner of Tyne Street. And Van der Schyff's still had the most beautiful materials! Each season the shop windows would be decorated differently. Before Eid, when the Muslims celebrate the end of their month-long daytime fast, the windows would be draped with brocades, satins and chiffon in the season's latest colours. At other times a dummy model would be dressed up as a bride, with flowing white bridal lace and her head gorgeously decorated with a veil. In her hand she would hold a lovely bouquet of plastic flowers.

We children would stand outside the shop window with our noses pressed up close against the glass and tell each other that that is how we would like to look when we got married one day.

Much of the material was imported, especially the rolls that were embroidered with gold and silver thread. These expensive materials were only bought by very rich Indian and Muslim people who came from all over the Cape.

The owner of Van der Schyff's was a Muslim gentleman who drove his sales ladies to work in his long, shiny, fancy car. They looked like royalty when they stepped out of the car because they were always dressed in the fashion of the day. These sales ladies were polite and friendly and it was well known that the prettiest sales ladies in District Six worked in Mr Van der Schyff's shop! The not so rich people never went into the shop because it looked so posh. They bought their materials at the cheaper Jewish stores of which there were many in Hanover Street.

Two other popular shops in District Six were "Stinkvis" and "Hannelaar" in Caledon Street.

Stinkvis was a nickname. From this shop you could buy all kinds of dried foodstuffs: beans, rice, dried peaches, pears, apples, apricots, prunes, raisins, mebos – plain and sugared. The shop was given its name because it had a fishy smell, probably from the dried fish that it also sold. Most of the supplies were stored in open hessian bags. The tops of the bags were rolled down, and as the supplies got fewer the bags would be rolled down lower and lower.

Stinkvis was often targeted by shoplifters. A group of children would enter, and one would keep the owner busy while the other little thieves quickly filled their pockets from the open bags. Sometimes Mr Stinkvis caught them, but most of the time the little ruffians managed to get away.

The name Hannelaar came from "handelaar" – trader – and he sold anything from straight sewing pins to dress material, extra large men's underwear to big ladies' bloomers. He also sold on tick and every Saturday after he had closed his shop you would find him walking through District Six with his walking stick and his little black book, doing his collecting.

15   Winnie and Blackie and
Jessie the cat lady

DISTRICT SIX WAS INFESTED WITH CATS, many of them strays. Cats roamed the area as if they owned it. It was a very good thing to own a cat or two in the District on account of the rats and mice with which the place was plagued.

We owned two cats: Winnie and Blackie. In winter, we children liked them to sleep at the bottom end of our beds because they would keep our feet nice and warm. Sometimes we would even fight over having the cats sleep with us! Winnie was the older cat. She had a thick, light grey coat and beautiful eyes that glowed in the dark. Blackie was her son. He was pitch black, with the same eyes as his mother. My mother adored both cats and when her housework was completed, we would take them to her and hold them on her lap where she checked them for fleas. Sometimes she would brush the fur out with a special brush.

Winnie was my mother's favourite and when she stroked her, Winnie would close her eyes, purr and fall asleep with a contented look on her face. Often when my mother sat with the cats on her lap like that I would sit at her feet and think to myself: why doesn't she hold and cuddle me like that? Maybe then I would also fall asleep on her lap.

But I knew it was impossible. I was such an active child, I would not have been able to sit still for long. And besides, I was much too big to be rocked to sleep by my mother. But in my next life, I always thought, I was going to request to be born as a cat. And yes, my name would be Winnie.

When our cat Winnie was in a happy mood and cleaned her face with her paws and licked herself all over, my mother would always say, "See, Winnie is cleaning herself. We can prepare ourselves for visitors." This was just one of her superstitions because we hardly ever got visitors. The only people who we considered visitors were those who knocked on the door, "mense van buite", who came from the Northern Suburbs or Athlone. Because my father had only one brother living "outside" District Six and my mother had no family at all, there was seldom a knock on the front door – our neighbours just walked in and were treated as family. The same was the case with close friends.

As we all grew up, Winnie got older and she spent more and more of her time sleeping, often outside the house. One day she didn't come home at all. The following morning, as soon as it became light, my dad went in search of her. He climbed onto the rooftop and found her "sleeping" peacefully in a corner where she must have died of old age. He carried her down and placed her on a small mat in our backyard.

All eight of us children cried bitterly. My mother was perhaps even sadder. She said Winnie was just like one of her children. That morning we all went to school with red eyes and heavy hearts. Winnie was going to be buried when we came home from school.

When we arrived home that afternoon, we all went straight to the backyard to say our last farewells to our beloved Winnie. My brothers Ron and Pete then wrapped her up in newspaper, put her in a tomato box and carried her to an open piece of land in between Aspeling and Pontac Street, close to the little green sub-station that used to be there, and buried her there. We called this place the "kraal", just like every one of the few open spaces in the District was called. In fact, even a very big open yard used to be called a "kraal".

Blackie, Winnie's son, missed her so much that he died soon afterwards. He was buried alongside his mother. These two cats were part of our family, but they were luckier than us children: unlike us, they were buried in the place where they were born.

Jessie "the cat lady" had a good job with a clothing manufacturer in Sir Lowry Road and she was always immaculately dressed in the most fashionable clothes, wearing beautiful scarves and at all times a matching bag and shoes.

Jessie was a spinster but she was a silk of a lady – an expression my mother used to say that someone was special and lovely. She rented a room from the Hassan family who occupied a house in Roger Street.

Every Friday after work Jessie would collect a standing order of minced meat from her butcher in Hanover Street. She bought the mince specially to feed the cats in our area. Come rain or sunshine, Jessie turned up every Friday afternoon in the lane behind our house. Here she would stand on tiptoe to reach onto the high wall where all the neighbourhood's cats were gathered.

The cats loved her. They turned up in different shapes and sizes, colours and temperaments. Some of them were rough and ugly, but when Jessie fed them, they all behaved like sweet, adorable kittens. In more ways than one she had them all eating out of her hand!

Jessie really had some kind of magic with cats. My sisters and I would time her on Friday afternoons. By five o'clock we would be waiting quietly by our backyard door for her arrival. We had to be very quiet so as not to cause a disturbance during "cat feeding time" because if we made a noise the cats would scatter and watch us from a distance. When it was quiet again, they would cautiously sneak back to Jessie.

There was this one grey-striped wild kind of a cat. He didn't belong to anybody and was terribly aggressive. My mother used to clean the fish in our backyard and in a matter of seconds this scary, wild little fellow would be sitting on the wall, growling in the hope that she would throw a scrap of fish in his direction. The longer it took Mom to notice him the louder he would growl, just like a wild cat. "Old Wild Cat" always upset me. I was really scared of him and once told Mom to throw him some sharp fish bones. She looked really shocked and said, "Penny, a person does not give sharp bones to any animal. It can get stuck in their throats and they could easily die. Under no circumstances should you give cats fish bones!"

But I didn't care whether he lived or died. To me he was just a wild cat, always fighting and hurting the other cats. But to my mother, who loved all animals, he was a cat like all the others, in

70

need of food and attention. Now the amazing thing about Old Wild Cat that I could never understand was that he was always on his very best behaviour when Jessie arrived on a Friday afternoon!

For years Jessie came to feed cats. Then one day we heard that one of the Hassan daughters was going to be married and Jessie's room would be needed for the new bride and groom. Jessie was forced to look for another place to stay. She found a room with friends of the Hassans in the Dry Docks at the top end of the District. Some people said this area, just below De Waal Drive, was called after the famous Docklands of London. Others said it was called "Dry Docks" because there were no bars on account of so many Muslims living there. But I always liked to believe that the name was inspired by the fabulous view of the Cape Town harbour from there.

Jessie invited my mother to visit her at her new place, so after she had settled in, my mother one evening took Shirley and me to pay Jessie a visit.

Jessie occupied an upstairs room with a full view of the docks. It had a very big window and we were fascinated by the scene in front of us. The docks were packed with large ships. Their lights shimmered in the distance. Downtown looked like a real fairyland. All through the visit Shirley and I sat in front of the window trying to count the lights, while my mother and Jessie talked. Suddenly we heard Jessie say to my mother that she liked her new home but that she did not know for how long she'd be allowed to live here. We pricked up our ears.

"Why are you talking in this way?" my mother asked.

"I heard my boss talking to his wife, telling her that he had heard District Six was going to be declared a white area."

There was a long silence, then my mother sighed and said, "We've also heard that rumour, Jessie. It will really be a sad day if it happens."

Shirley and I looked at each other. It was the first word we ever heard about any place being declared "a white area". We were worried, but soon we forgot about it because the grown-ups didn't talk about it again for a long time.

Jessie didn't stay in the Dry Docks for long. She moved somewhere else, but she did not let her moving interfere with the feeding of the cats. She continued to collect her mince from her butcher on a Friday after work, and after feeding them she would walk quite a distance to her new room in Adams Street.

A lot of people admired the way Jessie continued to feed the cats on Fridays. The same people who named her "the cat lady" now renamed her "the fairy godmother of the cats". They said it was amazing how the cats knew on which day she would come. How did they know which day was Friday?

But they knew, instinctively, and they'd faithfully gather on the wall of the service lane for the arrival of their beloved Jessie, even though some of the other cats had passed away and new ones had joined in.

The cats did not suspect anything, but sometimes when Shirley and I saw Jessie, we remembered the rumour that District Six was going to be declared "a white area".

16   High school

THE EDUCATION I GOT at Trafalgar High in Birchington Street was much better than the one Jane and I got at the primary schools we attended.

At my new school the work was much more, and now we had a different teacher for each subject. I was also forced to make new friends because Jane went to Zonnebloem, another high school.

I was much happier at Trafs, as we called it. At the time that I started writing this book, twenty-two years after I had left it, Trafs was still in existence and the same principal was still in charge!

It was at Trafalgar High that we youngsters became politically aware. For the first time we started to understand the situation we found ourselves in. Terrible rumours were going around: District Six was going to be demolished, and everybody would have to leave to make way for the whites.

Yet on the outside, life went on as before. People went to work as usual, and the older children went to school while the little ones stayed at home. People were pushing the dark cloud that was forming and growing by the day to the back of their minds. It seemed to me that reality was going to be faced only at the last moment, so I too continued to go to school like everyone else and did not give the pending matter much thought. Until one Saturday morning: I was passing Castle Bridge, the corner on Upper Darling Street and Sir Lowry Road, and was right outside the public toilets with the green railings opposite the YMCA, when a man stepped up to me, placed a sticker on my cardigan. A second man snapped a photograph of me.

I was taken by surprise and angry. They had no right to pin stickers on me, nor to take a photo! So without looking at it, I ripped the sticker from my cardigan and rushed down to town.

I never wore a scarf, but that day the table cloth was draping thickly over Table Mountain and the southeaster was blowing gale force, so I had tied my hair down with a pretty pink scarf with the Beatles printed on it which Aunty had given me. Because of that scarf the photographers mistook me for a young Muslim lady and the following week my picture was all over District Six on the front page of the Post newspaper.

I hadn't seen it but I was extremely upset when I heard about it and ran all the way from our house in Tyne Street to the office of the Post in Upper Darling Street. How dare they! I thought, they didn't have my permission to use the photograph and anyway, it's a lie to imply that I'm a Muslim!

On the way I met my brother Ron, coming down the road. He stopped and frowned and asked, "Why do you look so mad, and where are you rushing off to?"

"I'm on my way to sue the Post for putting my picture on their front page! Do you know that they made a mistake? They say I'm Muslim!"

Ron burst out laughing. "So what, everybody that knows us knows that you're not Muslim. And anyway, I saw the paper at work, and with that scarf on your head, who can blame those newspaper guys for mistaking you for one? Forget about the picture."

But I was determined to go to the newspaper's offices.

"Penny, come back here, there's nothing that you can do. News is news!" Ron shouted after me.

I took no notice of him and walked and half ran down Hanover Street until I got to the modern building where the offices were. There was nobody about. The front door was open so I looked on the board to see on which floor the Post was. Then I took the lift. When I finally found the offices, the door was locked. Everybody had left. Disappointed I walked back home.

My mother tried to console me but I was still upset. When Dad got home that evening he had a copy of the Post with him.

"It's a rather nice photo," he said. "We should frame it."

But I was not amused. "Everybody in the neighbourhood stops me to discuss the stupid picture," I complained.

"Have you read what is written underneath?" Dad asked.

74

The Post front cover that caused such consternation for Penny

I hadn't. Only then did I read the caption printed in large black letters:

MUSLIMS WARNED:
DON'T HELP DISTRICT SIX MOVE

Below the picture in small print it read:

THEY'RE PROUD TO BE DISTRICT SIXERS
A member of the District Six Defence Committee gives an "I am from District Six" sticker to a young woman. The committee has issued more than 20,000 stickers in its campaign to get people to identify themselves with District Six. Stickers were handed out outside all mosques on Sunday evenings and at Anglican churches in the morning.

The newspaper cost 5 cent and it was dated: March 6, 1966.

I felt sick. It was not a rumour any more. There it was in black and white: "All Muslims have been warned – on pain of "the Fire" – not to help carry out the removal of district six, which is to be declared a White area."

The use of my picture was nothing compared with this shock. I no longer wished to go down to the newspaper offices.

That weekend the article in the Post was the topic of discussion all over District Six. Some people said they were going to find somewhere else to live. They did not want trouble, nor were they going to wait for the government to come and remove them. Others said, "Don't worry, it'll still take years. Where will they put everybody? They must still build houses for us."

Nobody did anything. In our street nobody even did much objecting or fighting against what was about to happen. My mother said, "We won't stand a chance against the government. We have been paying rent all these years and we were never given the opportunity to buy our homes. My parents paid rent to the same owners for thirty-five, and we've been paying rent for another twenty-five years – a total of sixty years. This house has been paid for over and over. What's the use of fighting for something that isn't even yours!"

Some people in District Six owned their houses, but I knew that most of the property belonged to Jewish landlords who did not want to sell their property to coloured people. Often they were not even prepared to talk to their tenants, let alone come to have a look at the place! And if the landlords did get around to doing any kind of renovation, the rent just went up.

So the properties were left to deteriorate more and more, giving the government more and more of an excuse to move out the people living there.

After that article in the Post, many write-ups about District Six appeared in other newspapers. But still most people just adopted Aunty Moena's attitude, who said: "I'm too old and tired to fight. All I can do is wait and see what'll happen." (Aunty Moena lived in Parkin Street. She was also forced to leave – a year after we were.)

17   The southeaster

I NEVER LIKED THE WIND. It frightened me and I always wished it away. I imagined that the roof of our house was going to blow off and that the walls would come tumbling down on us.

We were five children sleeping in one room, and as a little girl I had nightmares that we would all be covered with bricks and stones, sand and dust in such a storm. I feared the corrugated roof sheeting most. What if this fell down on us? We would all be dead and nobody would find us under all that debris! When the wind howled like a wild animal, I would sit up and watch the walls and imagine I saw them moving.

Sometimes when I placed my hands on the wall behind my bed, I could actually feel it vibrate. But from the time that I was a little girl to when I was grown up, not one of our roof sheets ever blew off, nor did any of the walls ever come tumbling down on us. I could have saved myself all my fears and nightmares. But to this day I still do not like the southeaster.

One day, when Shirley and I were teenagers, we decided to go swimming at the Sea Point tidal pool. My mother, who had just returned from her Saturday shopping trip, noticed that the south-easter was slowly spreading its cloth all across the top of Table Mountain. It wouldn't be long before it arrived down in District Six. "Why don't you postpone your swimming trip?" she asked. "Rather go and see Gone with the Wind, it's playing at the Avalon. Clark Gable is in it." Gable was her favourite actor.

"Mom, is it not enough that the southeaster is going to blow? Why you suggesting that we should go and see a film called Gone with the Wind on top of it?" Shirley said.

"Listen, girls, there's no comparison between that film and our wind, and everybody should go and see that film at least once in their lifetime."

"Why, Mom?"

"Just go and see it, and you'll find out for yourselves what the film is all about."

After a lot of debate we eventually left the house, walked to the Avalon on the corner of Russell and Hanover Streets, and bought our tickets. We both loved the sad story of Scarlett O'Hara, played by Vivien Leigh, and when the last image faded away, we both said we'd like to watch it again some day. Slowly we got up and walked to the exit. We had completely forgotten about the southeaster.

A cold wind hit us in the face. We staggered back inside. People had gathered in front of the Avalon to button up their jerseys. The ladies were tying up their scarves before they set off for home. Shirley and I looked at each other, linked arms and made a run for it.

As we crossed Russell Street a gust of wind grabbed us, rushed us across and pushed us into the wall of a shop in Hanover Street. We felt like two drunkards falling about. My arm was aching from the way Shirley was holding it.

Two men had to come and help us up.

"Thank you," we said. "We're fine, we're just scared of the wind." We linked arms again and made a fresh dash for home. We half ran and half floated through the air the way the southeaster was sweeping us along. Eventually we made it home in one piece but rather jittery on our legs. The wind chased us right into the passage. My mother ran to see why we had burst, and not walked, in through the front door.

"Is the devil after you?" she asked.

"No, Mom, the southeaster!" we laughed.

Aunty, who lived with us, never left the house when the wind blew hard. She had an even greater fear of the wind than I, because she'd once had a very bad experience with the southeaster.

She was rather skinny when she was young, she told us. On her way from work one day in November many years ago, she came up Caledon Street, and it was here that a gust of wind picked her up, blew her down Tennant Street and over into Hanover, where it threw her right in front of a car. Luckily for her, it was a parked car.

"Did anybody see how the wind blew you?" I asked her.

"I didn't notice anybody. On gale-force days people stay indoors, and anyway, I couldn't turn my head. The only way I could stop blowing down the street was to grab onto one of the tyres of that parked car. I was still crouching and clinging to the tyre when a passer-by stopped to help me. I was too frightened to let go for fear of being blown away again. The man assured me that he would help me and that I must let go. I eventually did and the man half carried me here."

The moment my mother saw Aunty's condition she apparently sent one of us over to the babbie to ask him to phone for an ambulance. The ambulance men took one look at Aunty and said they would have to take her to Woodstock Hospital. The driver wanted to know who had attacked her like that.

"Nobody touched her," my mother explained. "The damage was done by the southeaster."

The driver looked at my mother in disbelief, Aunty said. They carried her into the ambulance strapped to a stretcher. My mother accompanied her to the hospital. Fortunately the wind had died down by then.

"The doctor sent me for X-rays and it was discovered that besides the bruises I had two broken ribs and a fractured wrist! The day after the accident both my eyes were black and swollen. I looked and felt too terrible!"

A much more tragic accident happened in District Six because of the southeaster. A corrugated roof sheet was blown off a roof at the very moment that a young Muslim lady left her front door in Chapel Street to visit family in Caledon Street. Just as she was about to close the door, the roof sheet hit her right on the head.

She was killed instantly. Her parents were dumb struck. The one minute she was in the house, and the next she was taken away from them.

The family and other people found it unbelievable that someone so young and beautiful was killed in this way. It was one of the greatest personal tragedies in the history of District Six. The young lady was buried the following day, and Muslim and Christian people came from all over District Six to pay their respects to the family.

Of course, at the time of her burial there was not a breath of wind!

There were times when the southeaster blew for seven days on end. This made the grown-ups short-tempered and the children miserable. Small children were not allowed to play outside. Not only because it was unpleasant and dangerous, but some superstitious people believed that there were devils roaming about in the wind. The evil spirits would be especially active when the cannon on Signal Hill went off at twelve o'clock. It was also believed that the devils preferred to settle on small children and babies. For this reason, mothers were warned not to stand in the doorway with a baby in their arms when the wind blew. And if a baby was restless that night, this was blamed on the devils in the wind.

The skollies of District Six called the southeaster "die wilde wyfiewind" – the wild female wind. The world-famous name for it is of course the "Cape doctor". To this day, after the wind has settled, the whole of Cape Town is clean.

District Six certainly always looked after a strong wind as if someone had just swept it with a giant broom. Calm would be restored, the mothers would once again sit outside on their stoeps or on the pavement, and the children could once again be seen playing in the streets.

18 Films, cinemas and old buildings

THERE WERE FOUR CINEMAS in District Six, all within walking distance of each other.

The Avalon was the most select and here the more modern films were shown. It was always a pleasure to go and watch a film at the Avalon because no ruffians or "bad elements" were allowed in. It was especially famous for showing Indian films with subtitles. The whole of the Avalon would be booked out by our primary school if a special film was shown, and I saw Mother India, The Ten Commandments, Boot Polish, The Good Earth, Ben Hur, The Big Fisherman and many more great films there with my best friend Jane.

The entrance to the Star bioscope was in Hanover Street, right opposite the fish market. The side entrance was opposite St Mark's Church in Clifton Street. To watch a film from upstairs in the Star was alright, but one had to be brave to go in and take a seat downstairs.

Doctor Zhivago, starring Omar Sharif, was showing and I wanted to see it very badly. I had left school by then and was working. I didn't want to go alone to the Star, so I asked my mom if she would go with me, but she refused, saying, "You know I never go to places like that because the smoking gives me asthma."

Ron was going out and Shirley had to study. It was the last time that Doctor Zhivago was going to be shown and I had no option but to ask my dad – I even offered to pay for his ticket! He never went to the cinema as he preferred to read books, so I was very surprised when he agreed to accompany me.

When we arrived at the Star, the upstairs seats were all booked out. Only two seats were still available downstairs and they were right in front.

"What shall we do?" I asked my dad.

"We may as well buy the tickets and stay to watch the film."

It was unbearable sitting right in front. The smell of the dagga being smoked at the back drifted down there and the people around us were making a lot of noise, some using obscene language.

I tried very hard to concentrate on the film. I was getting more and more scared of sitting there and wanted to tell my dad that we should leave, but he seemed to be enjoying himself. I consoled myself with the thought that no harm would come to us while he was there, especially as the surroundings did not seem to bother him much. I tried to relax, but it was impossible not to feel uncomfortable: fleas or bugs had started to bite my legs!

The film eventually did end and it was a relief to be outside in the fresh night air again.

On the way home Dad said, "I never again want to hear that any of my children, including you, wish to go to the Star. Even if you can get seats upstairs. The place has changed so much over the years, I had no idea that the patrons could now do just as they pleased."

Maybe it was a good thing after all that we went that night, though, because the Star burnt down soon afterwards.

Right from the start, my dad did not allow us to go the British bio-scope in Caledon Street, just around the corner from the National Theatre in William Street. It was considered too rough by most parents. Young guys were always hanging out in front of the British and sometimes one could see them gambling on the steps.

I used to think that the National Theatre must have attracted select audiences in the distant past, for the theatre building with its fancy architecture looked rather out of place among the houses of William Street.

Here too we preferred to sit upstairs, watching scary films like Zorro, The Hunchback of Notre Dame, Chalk Garden, Dracula and Frankenstein. Also The Phantom of the Opera. Jane and I went to the five o'clock show. When we came out it was dark and we were both scared stiff. We ran home as fast as we could, imagining the Phantom was after us. That evening we made an oath never to go and watch horror movies again.

In Hanover Street there were many old buildings, some of them without any electricity. Different kinds of people lived in these buildings – "select" people, average families, and gangsters all lived next to each other, and all hung their washing from the balconies. There was no other place. Couples who got married moved in with their families and new babies were born and grew up here. The elderly passed away and younger people took their places. People of all colours and creeds lived side by side. Sometimes a fight would break out, but when it was settled, things would just go back to normal. Here and there a brilliant child would manage to study in these conditions. He or she would finish school and end up being someone of importance. Everyone in District Six would respect such a person.

One building in particular always interested me: Hanover Building opposite the Rose & Crown Bar. This building was very tall and it had the most beautiful stucco around the top. The balconies looked so daintily odd against the stark ugliness of the surrounding cardboard and corrugated sheeting structures and the washing lines with their eternal washing hanging out to dry in the breeze. Buses, cars, horses and carts, bicycles and people all buzzed past in the street below.

I spent quite a lot of time opposite Hanover Building because my father spent quite a lot of time inside the Rose & Crown, and my mother always sent me to go and call him if there was someone to see him. I hated this.

Because I was a girl I was not allowed to go into the bar, so I had to wait outside and ask the first man on his way into the bar to please tell my father that his daughter Penny was outside waiting for him. Dad always took his time to come out.

It was while I had to wait for him that I used to look at Hanover Building. By now it was well known that District Six was going to be declared a white area. I felt sad to think that this beautiful old building, together with so many well-constructed homes, would soon be demolished.

If my dad took particularly long to make his appearance, the guys that walked past the bar would pass comments about my standing there, and so, to take my mind off an unpleasant situation, I stood there and daydreamed.

If this building stood in Sea Point it would be looked at in a different light, I would think. If only the landlord could revamp and clean it!

I had hundreds of ideas of what could be done. I was only a teenager then and would imagine that I was a tourist taking photographs of this lovely, renovated place to show my friends back home in England or whatever. If only the City Council or someone would see the beauty in this building and repair it! Or maybe the tenants could be asked to hang their washing in the backyard instead of over the balconies. It would already look so much better. Why couldn't they rather put up window boxes and fill them with geraniums or petunias like in Austria?

In my imagination I saw all kinds of wonderful possibilities for the building. At the entrance one could place two large flower pots ... oh, I used to think, Hanover Street would be so attractive if it was cleaned up. All the skollies and loafers would automatically improve themselves and tourists would come from all over the world to see how we all lived together peacefully in District Six. New Year would be the best of all times! The Cape Coons' Carnival with its brightly coloured satins, umbrellas, painted faces, singsongs and the general feeling of wellbeing and fun would swing through District Six, down to Adderley Street and Green Point, and everyone would be enjoying themselves.

For our row of semi-detached cottages in Tyne Street I pictured white walls, yellow shutters, doors and window frames, and tall flowering shrubs in big white pots on either side of the front doors – with shiny brass door handles and letterbox covers.

I would step out of my dream the moment my dad appeared from the Rose & Crown, and then the two of us would walk home hand in hand.

"Dad," I said one day, "I'm getting too big now to be standing outside a bar waiting for you. You must tell Mom to send one of the boys to fetch you. But," I added, "the problem can be solved if you stay away from that place."

"Look, Penny," he said, "I like going there sometimes. That's where one picks up all kinds of information."

With that I couldn't argue. Dad probably first heard about the government's plans for District Six in the Rose & Crown.

19 Roetie the hairdresser and the Indian brothers' barber shop

S HE WAS MOST LIKELY christened Ruth and might have been nicknamed Ruthy, but everyone knew her as "Roetie".

She lived in a corner house in Parkin Street with her mother, sister, brother and two small girls and operated a hairdressing ser-

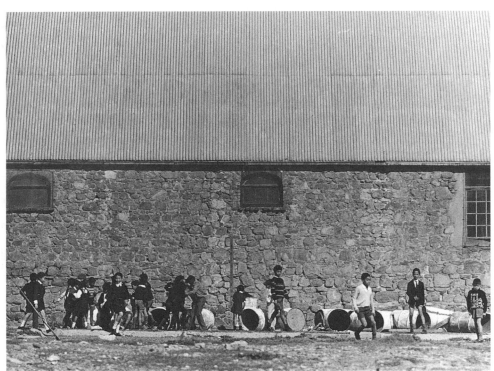

J H Greshoff

J H Greshoff

Above: St Marks in Tennant Street, one of the many primary schools which the children of District Six attended from standard three to five. Schools were not always gentle places of education, and occasionally a lively scrap between an irate parent and a bad tempered teacher was enjoyed by both pupils and passers-by.

Just posing. Although strictly prohibited and punishable by the most severe methods, youths remained intrigued by smoking and many secretly indulged in the habit.

Cloete Breytenbach

Cloete Breytenbach

Facing page: Tweede Nuwe Jaar belonged to the "Coon" Carnaval troupes, here pouring down Hanover Street in their bright satins, white shoes and Panama hats. A marching stick and frilly umbrella completed the outfit. Each troupe wore distinctive colours and was accompanied by its own marching band, which usually included banjos, guitars, saxophones and tambourines.

Above: Bystanders could not resist joining in in the fun of the New Year celebrations. Neither could this troupie, with his characteristically painted face, resist leaving the ranks for a quick hug – which would leave the lady with black Nugget and white Shoeshine smudges on her cheek.

Next page: In the fifties, before the disintegration of the buildings and the community started, a wedding was a grand affair. Here, one of the offspring of the well-known Schroeder Muslim family is getting married. Amidst interested onlookers the couple, assisted by the father, a best man and flower girl, is setting off in a hansom cab drawn by a horse, also reared in the District.

Omar Collection

vice from her home. Her speciality was straightening ladies' hair. Though it was never said aloud everyone knew that some men also came to her in secret to have their hair treated.

Her house, which appeared huge from the outside, stood a bit higher than the houses around it. One had to go up four steps to get to the front door, which was left open most of the time.

Roetie was one of a kind in her field of hairdressing. People made appointments well in advance. Her customers, who lived as far afield as Worcester, Paarl and Wellington, would write a letter to say when they would arrive. They came by train to Cape Town Station and then walked up to her house from there.

Roetie's "hairdressing salon" was operated from her large entrance hall. This was a square room of approximately twelve feet by twelve feet, with chairs placed all along the walls.

Except for those who had made special appointments, her ladies were attended to on a first come, first serve basis. When the weather was hot, Roetie's ladies would sit outside on the steps and the small children in the neighbourhood would gather around to stare at them.

In one corner of the entrance hall was a long wooden table. On this table a burning primus stove stood, ready for the iron combs with their heat-resistant handles which Roetie heated on the ring of the stove. There were several jars of Vaseline on a shelf next to the table. While Roetie was busy with a customer, the peculiar smell of oil on hot iron and hair would float on the air outside.

Roetie always followed the same procedure. First she placed a clean towel over the shoulders of her customer, then she combed the lady's hair out with a wide-toothed plastic comb. When she was satisfied with the state of the hair, she took an iron comb from the stove and immediately placed another on the ring. She would wipe the hot comb with a cloth before she treated the customer's Vaselined hair strand by strand. Patiently Roetie combed in the "curls" and "waves" with the hot iron comb, styling the lady's hair according to her wishes. When she had finished, Roetie would tell her lady to look in the big mirror on the wall above the wooden table.

The ladies always beamed with happiness. Roetie's bonus to her clients was a tube of ruby lipstick, which she encouraged them to put on their lips then and there, before they left her salon.

For a wedding, the bride's and bridesmaids' hair was often straightened. The little flower girls loved it when Roetie styled their straightened hair into smooth curls on top of their heads by rolling the curls around her forefinger and placing them in position with a hairclip. Small flowers were usually fitted inside each curl.

Roetie worked alone and she made good money from her trade. The poorer parents had to save money for quite a while before they could afford to send a daughter to her, and the more daughters there were, the more it cost the parents. Young girls who didn't have straight hair would often choose a "straightening treatment" from Roetie as a birthday present, especially when they turned twenty-one and a party was held for them in the community hall.

Even if Roetie never touched your hair you could see that her hands were smooth and soft from all the Vaseline that she had been using over the years.

For men there were many barber shops in District Six to choose from. My father had gone to the same barber shop for as long as he could remember: the two Indian brothers in Tennant Street just off Hanover Street. Both Jeewa brothers were married and had children and the two families shared a house higher up in Roger Street.

The children tended the same school as we. They were very

reserved and always polite. Sometimes one of the younger boys would sneak out to play with my brother Colin. The minute she missed him, his mother, who was always dressed in a sari and rarely left the house, would come looking for her son. Like the young Mrs Jeewa, the whole Indian community in District Six were very protective of their children, and they were hardly ever allowed to play out of doors.

The Indian brothers were gentlemen in the true sense of the word and they were respected by their neighbours as well as their patrons. They both wore hats and were always neatly dressed, sporting a collar and tie every day. Their barber shop was less than a five minutes' walk from Roger Street and they had to pass our house on their way to work in the mornings. They would always tilt their hats ever so slightly and nod their heads whenever any of us was around.

The Jeewa brothers could hardly speak Afrikaans, the language of many people in District Six, but they did their best to understand what their clients wanted. Hairstyles for young men and boys changed continually and they must have had a hard time keeping up with the trends of the time and the demands of their customers.

As my brothers grew up, they too had their hair cut there.

It was always my duty as the eldest daughter to take Colin to the barber shop. My mother did not have the patience to sit and wait in line with him, so she sent me instead. It is never a pleasant experience when a barber attempts to cut a small boy's hair. With Colin it was particularly bad. He hated to have his hair cut and sometimes he would fight and scream in the shop. I used to ask my mother to give me some money for sweets so that I could bribe him to sit still in the barber's chair. Whenever he misbehaved I would slip him a sweet and then he would sit quietly for a short while. But a minute or two later he'd start wriggling again and take the sweet out of his mouth. It would be covered in fine hairs. Then he would cry, and so the poor barber could not get on with the job of cutting his hair.

Sometimes the kind, younger Jeewa brother who always cut Colin's hair would leave him for a while to settle down and then come back to start all over again. There were other times when I ran out of sweets and very quietly slipped out of the barber shop to buy some more at the shop next door. The second Colin discovered I was gone, he'd jump out of the chair to look for me. It was an impossible situation and my patience would begin to run out. The young Mr Jeewa could see that I was getting agitated.

"Be calm, young lady," he often said to me. "I have all the experience in the world with little boys. You'll see, just a few more minutes and you can go home."

"Colin, now get back in the chair," he would then say in his firm yet gentle manner. Colin always obeyed and allowed the barber to continue and I would think to myself that this man must be some kind of saint to have so much patience!

At last the barber would put down his comb and scissors and reach for the brush. Brushing the loose hair from Colin's face and neck he would say, "See, Colin, that wasn't so bad after all. You have been a very good customer."

From where he was standing next to the barber's chair in the middle of the room, he would reach across the small counter where the money was kept and hand Colin a small Nestlé chocolate. "This is for you, Colin, so that you can come back to me when you next need a haircut."

With the chocolate clutched tightly in his hand and a broad grin on his face, Colin would look at the barber, not saying a word, but in his eyes I could see that my little brother would be back for his next haircut, if only to be rewarded with a chocolate at the end.

Colin's behaviour at the barber shop improved as he grew

90

older. Until he one day said to me that it was no longer necessary for me to take him. He could go by himself. Mom disagreed as he was only six years old. It was too dangerous for him to cross Hanover Street all by himself, she said. "Think of all the traffic and buses."

I had to agree with her and went along with Colin. The barber was happy to see us. He told me to take a seat and told Colin to get into the barber's chair, which he did without hesitation.

"This will be Colin's last haircut at this barber shop," Mr Jeewa suddenly said. "My brother and I will be leaving soon."

"Leaving?" I asked.

"Yes. We have been served with eviction papers. Tennant Street and the whole block is going to be demolished."

"Have you found another barber shop?" I asked, not knowing what else to say.

"We can do nothing with another barber shop in District Six. We have been given papers saying that we should go and live in an Indian area."

The older brother, who hardly ever spoke, was clearly not himself and almost shouted, "Indian indeed! We have lived up there in Roger Street for all these years. All our children were born here in the area. Do you know where the Peninsula Maternity home is?"

I nodded. The maternity home was just across Tennant Street near the bottom of Caledon Street.

"That is where our children were born. Your father, we know him for half of his life. We remember, it was during the Second World War that he married your mother. For years and years he came to our barber shop and then over the years your four brothers also started coming here. Oh, it is no use complaining. To whom can we complain? Nobody will listen to us. Those white men, they just handed us the papers and told us to be gone within two months."

I just sat there, speechless. This meant that maybe we would be next to be told to go. Where would we go? I sat there with my heart in my throat.

When Colin and I got home, Dad had already arrived back from work. I greeted him and mentioned casually that the two Jeewa brothers were closing their barber shop soon, and that he and my brothers would have to go to another barber in the future.

I immediately regretted bursting the news on him like that because it upset him terribly. He started pacing around the kitchen, criticising the government and condemning the Group Areas Act.

"Wait till they come and kick us out! I'll tell them exactly what's on my mind!" he shouted.

The Group Areas officials did not visit us as we expected them to do. They wanted the Indians out first.

20 Changing times

OVER THE YEARS, things changed at home. Because of ill health Dad stopped working at the garage in Roeland Street. He also didn't do much spare work, but he still often went cray-fishing. And if he did not go to the sea, he would visit his friends in Roger Street – Mr Jimmy la Guma and Mr O'Connell. Except for these two friends, he never went into anybody else's home because he preferred to spend his time with his family or at the Rose & Crown.

These three gentlemen had many views in common, especially

when they were discussing politics. They would get very heated up about the government's racial discrimination and about discrimination in education. They spoke about the Immorality Act and unfair labour practices. Dad got particularly upset about all the white immigrants who arrived in the country poor and got the best jobs, after they had to be taught by "non-whites" – people who could do the jobs but by law weren't allowed to do so.

We could not help but listen, although children, even teenagers, dared not take part in the conversation. It was strictly grown-up business.

Dad's other interests were reading and listening to the radio. As he got sicker he started to spend more and more time in bed.

Finally, after we had been expecting it for a long time, the "Group Areas", as everybody called the officials who had to see to it that this Act was put into practice, came around to check up on how many people were living in our house.

"I won't speak to them," Dad told Mom when she went to the bedroom to call him. "I'd rather die first before I would speak to them."

Mom had no option but to give the men the details. They left and we did not see them for quite a while.

Slowly people started to move away from District Six.

"We're not moving," Dad said. "If anybody wants me and my family to move it will have to be over my dead body!"

We didn't realise that these were prophetic words.

Aunty had also changed. As we grew older she could no longer beat us. She became calmer and when the house had its quieter moments, she and Mom would sit and talk together for hours, and one would get the impression that they really were sisters. But Aunty was always the stronger one and she still had the power to manipulate my mother.

And then a serious quarrel erupted between Aunty and my dad and he threw her out of our house.

In a way it was fortunate, because we needed her room desperately. By this time we were three teenagers in the house, and we immediately changed the front room into a bed-sitting room.

Aunty went to live with a couple in Wicht Street. Mrs Abrahams was young and needed someone to take care of her two small children while she worked as a model and a clerk in a clothing factory in Sir Lowry Road. Aunty agreed to look after the kids. We did not see much of her, but for the rest, life went on as before.

Then one Friday afternoon, Jessie, the "fairy godmother of the cats", failed to arrive. The hours passed and the cats waited and waited. They all lingered, clearly hoping that she was merely delayed.

But Jessie never turned up to feed them. We were worried, so in the end my mother went to Adams Street, where she was living when we last saw her, to find out what had happened to her. The house where the Tofiek family used to live was deserted.

Some people later said that when they last saw Jessie, she was looking very sad and upset. She would not speak to anybody, just kept on mumbling, "Who will feed my cats, who will feed my cats?"

Like the Jeewa brothers and the many other people who had already been forced to leave District Six, so the cats also had to go. Some families took their cats with them, but many cats were left behind to fend for themselves. I picked up a little stray outside Banks Hiring Supply one Saturday afternoon and took it home. I called it Sweety.

After that, rumours started going around that Jessie had been spotted feeding the cats. Some of the people who were still living in District Six swore that one could on a Friday afternoon sometimes catch a glimpse of a silhouette standing up on tiptoe to feed the cats on the wall.

Many Friday afternoons around five we looked out for the silhouette. We never saw it. It made us sad, because even today, many years after the service lane and all the houses in Tyne and Godfrey Streets have been demolished, some people still say that Jessie and her cats can sometimes be seen on that spot on a Friday afternoon.

21 Shebeens and "select" people

THERE WERE MANY SHEBEENS in District Six. There was one in our street as well, on the corner of Roger Street, opposite Kader's shop. It was in a double-storey inhabited by "Natives" and everyone called it "The Building".

Downstairs was the shebeen, and upstairs the "select" people lived.

The select people were better off and did not mix much with the people downstairs. Select people were caring and respectable and dressed smartly. They didn't drink or behave foolishly or make noise.

At that time, African people were not allowed to buy wine and so their shebeens had what was called a "mailer", someone of a lighter skin colour who bought the liquor for them.

The mailer of the shebeen in Tyne Street was a man known by the name of Whitey, and he had a dog called Bullit. Because only Africans lived in The Building, Whitey, who was in fact "Coloured", lived somewhere in Sidney Street.

The Building after it was turned into Ghiwala's Eastern Gem Spice factory

Whitey was well paid for his work. During the day he walked from off-sales to off-sales to buy wine, because at the time "Coloureds" were also only allowed a certain quota of wine per day. If you bought more than that quantity you had to sign a register.

All the bar owners knew Whitey as he brought them lots of business, and they didn't always make him sign the register.

Friday nights, the shebeen people really performed. Fights broke out and regularly exploded right out into the street in front of The Building. Someone always called the police and in no time everyone would be outside to see the action. The Law regularly raided the place and if they found wine, they poured it out into the street.

The "main guy" of the shebeen was a fat lady who always wore black. She would object loudly and try to stop the police from pouring out her bottles and bottles of wine. Sometimes the Law would load her into the back of the van, but within a day or two she was out of jail again. People used to say that she had a "connection" at the jail up in Roeland Street, which was why she was never kept there for long.

After a visit from the Law all would be quiet for a week or two, and then faithful Whitey could be seen again with his big bag on his way back from the bottle stores to deliver the goods to The Building, Bullit following him like a shadow.

When the ordinary bars and bottle stores were closed, the men – and some women – would find their way to the shebeens. So during weekends and public holidays the shebeens made lots of money. Sometimes the shebeen owner would sell wine on tick, and at the end of the week the liquor had to be paid for.

There were times when a man would make so much debt at the shebeen that it amounted to a whole week's wages. His family would have no money left for food. Neighbours often made contributions to help the family out, because in District Six everybody knew everybody's business as we all lived so close together. If people had food left over, it was common practice to send it over to those who did not have enough. You never needed to starve; all you had to do was ask.

One Monday morning, an old Muslim lady whom everybody called Ouma went to pay a visit to the wife of a man who had once again spent all his money at the shebeen. The wife, a regular church-goer, forbade her husband to bring even a drop of wine into the house. Ouma said to her that she, Ouma, had heard the husband only drank over weekends, and never during the week.

"Think about it," Ouma patiently explained, "if you allowed him to bring a bottle or two home over the weekend, there would be no reason for him to go to the shebeen. Look, your husband is one of the people who make the shebeen-owners rich. A stop should be put to it."

It was very strange for Ouma to have given her such advice, as drinking is strictly forbidden to all Muslims, but the wife took the old lady's advice and within a few weeks there was an improvement in the family's living conditions. In the end, the husband even went to church with his wife on Wednesday evenings!

Lindiwe was one of the select people and with her mother, father and two brothers lived upstairs in The Building. They were a well-respected family. I was friends with Lindiwe, and her brothers Mac and James were friends with Ron as we all grew up in the same street.

Lindiwe's mother worked in service and sometimes she and my mother would talk outside when she passed our house on her way back to The Building. I loved to listen to her because she had a soft voice with a lovely lilting accent.

Lindiwe's father was a real gentleman. Mr Mtwa was always dressed in a dark suit, his shoes shone at all times, and he was never without his briefcase. When he passed the ladies in the street, he tilted his hat ever so gently and greeted them very politely. Mom used to say he was just like the men who acted in the American movies. He had style and sophistication.

Mr Mtwa's sons were allowed to play outside, but not his daughter. She was brought up like a lady.

Lindiwe and I often visited each other, mostly over the weekends. To get to their rooms you had to enter through the ground floor of The Building and walk up a rickety staircase which had a step or two missing. I had to be careful going up as the stairs were open at the back and if you looked down you could glimpse the floor between the stairs. And it was always dark as The Building had no electricity connection. Instead candles and lamps were used.

The moment you reached the top of the stairs, things changed. Light streamed onto the landing from the open windows. Lindiwe would welcome me and the two of us would disappear into her room. The Mutwas occupied the whole top floor so she, her parents and her brothers all had their own rooms. We spent all our time in her room. She had many books and magazines. She loved reading and was always studying and doing her school work. She wanted to be somebody special one day, like a doctor, and not a domestic servant like her mother, she said.

"I know I'll have to work very hard, because there won't be many opportunities for us in future. My parents can't even leave the house now without their passes," she said one afternoon, looking out of the window at the street below. "That's why I want to learn and earn a lot of money one day – to take them to America. There they won't have to carry a pass."

On my way out that afternoon, Lindiwe gave me some magazines to take home with me, as she always did. But I didn't open them for the whole week. I was too upset by the look on her face when she told me about her plans for the future.

Ron and the Mutwa boys did different things together. They went for rides on their bikes and swam at Trafalgar Baths in Searle Street. And some winter evenings, they would take an old paraffin tin with holes punched into the sides and make a fire inside. This "galley" was for boys only, and no girls were allowed near it.

Ron sometimes took potatoes from the kitchen or bought "penny polony" from Motjie Kader. Then the boys would put the potato or meat on sticks and roast it over the fire. Mac and James had a portable radio, which they always brought along, and the three would prance around the fire to the music of LM Radio.

One day in the winter of 1966, Aunty unexpectedly came into the kitchen where my mother and I were busy and said she had just heard that all the "Natives" were going to be removed. They could no longer live among the "Coloureds", not to mention in the "White area" that District Six was supposed to become. She did not know when this was to happen, but it was going to be soon.

It happened sooner than anyone had expected. The one evening we still saw our African friends and neighbours, and the following morning The Building was completely empty. All the places in Tyne Street where Africans used to live were deserted – The Building opposite Kader's shop, the open plot next to it, as well as the house next door. All were empty.

We were flabbergasted, until someone mentioned that the government trucks arrived during the night and that they managed to remove the people before daybreak.

The Mtwas' neighbours and friends were in a state of shock. All day people talked. Some were so upset that they did not even go to work. I couldn't understand why Lindiwe had not come to say goodbye to us, and so was Ron.

"Damn this government and its laws!" my dad cursed. "The day will come when they will regret what they are doing to District Six. They want to eradicate us completely by demolishing the area. The day will come when the whole bloomin' lot of them will have to pay for their selfishness."

Mom had to calm him down and tell him not to speak like that in front of us children.

Lindiwe didn't leave a forwarding address. For a long time I wondered if the people knew where they were being taken to.

22 Old Sunny Boy

NOBODY KNEW HIS REAL NAME or even his surname. He was known by everyone in District Six as "Old Sunny Boy" and you could always recognise him, even from far off: he was tall of build, always wore a hat, and his clothes were specially tailor-made – the jacket a little longer than it should be and the pants just a bit wider than normal. Most of the time he wore a pair of black and white shoes.

During the day, Old Sunny Boy was employed as a messenger by a large insurance company in Darling Street. Then he did not wear his fancy clothes – he had to wear a uniform with a special hat bearing the company's emblem.

The moment Old Sunny Boy came home from work, he changed into his nice clothes. He lived in Wicht Street, but he always hung out at the babbie shop on the corner of Tennant and Chapel Streets. For he had a special talent: he could sing any song and do imitations of all the original artists. So as soon as his chums joined him, they would say, "Hey, hey there, Old Sunny Boy, how about a song for your old chummies? What will it be today – ol' Frankie? Or how about a Nat King Cole?"

Then Old Sunny Boy would say, "No, man, can't you guys see that it's a bit cold, and look there, man, that blanket is again thick on old Table Mountain. Let's get that paraffin tin and make a fire first to get warm."

With the sun setting and the fire blazing, what more did a man need to start singing?

"Hey, come on now, Old Sunny Boy," his friend Knockies would shout. His real name was Brian, but everybody called him Knockies because of his knock knees.

"You blokes must stop calling me Old Sunny Boy," Old Sunny Boy would say. "I'm not old, my name is Old Sunny Boy. And besides, how do you expect a man to sing with a thirst? You know that I'm not allowed to bring the good stuff into the house, the old lady will throw me out. So come, come, guys, pass on the refreshment."

Chicken always brought the drink hidden in the inside pocket of his jacket. His name was Chicken because his hair was very straight and the front had the habit of falling forward, just like the comb of a cock. Chicken's father ran a shebeen in Hanover Street and Chicken used to say that when his old man was not around, he just helped himself to a bottle as it was for a good cause – like entertainment.

Whenever you went to Solly's shop on the corner of Tennant and Chapel Streets in the late afternoon, you could hear the singing. Old Sunny Boy had a beautiful voice and he loved to sing songs like the one on his namesake Sunny Boy, or Three Coins in the Fountain, White Christmas, Moon River, They Tried to Tell Us We're too Young and When Irish eyes are Smiling. His friends joined in the chorus, clicking their fingers and swaying to the music. If he was too hoarse, Chicken would whistle along.

Old Sunny Boy was often invited to sing for shows, but he always refused.

"Why?" Knockies asked him. "You got the talent. You can make it anywhere."

But Old Sunny Boy said that he was a throw-away child and he would never leave the old lady who took him in and had looked after him since birth. His own mother left him to run off with a Japanese sailor. He was scared of being famous, he said, and so refused all offers to stardom. He had no intention to leave his old lady, as she was getting on in years. Had she not worked hard to keep him at school, and when he finished his schooling got him the job at the insurance company? Now she was not well enough to work any longer. "I made a vow to myself that I will look after the old lady till the end because she loves me better than any mother could ever love a child."

Once I was sent to Solly's shop to buy some fresh mebos and dried fruit. Solly was known to sell only the best quality. To get inside I had to pass the singer and his gang. Being shy I hurried into the shop, bought the mebos and dried fruit, paid and prepared to leave. But it was no use: on my way out Old Sunny Boy burst into "There goes my heart, there goes the one I l-o-v-e".

"And now, why's the young lady blushing like that?" Chicken shouted.

I knew that Old Sunny Boy and his friends flirted like this with all the girls that came to the shop, but I still broke into a run to get away.

Aunty knew Old Sunny Boy's "old lady", as he referred to her. She was a widow and her real name was Mrs Simpson. Her husband passed away when Old Sunny Boy was only eighteen months old. One day Aunty visited Sunny's mother, like she'd sometimes do before she left. Mrs Simpson, who must have been close to seventy years at the time, told Aunty that Sunny recently got more offers to sing. Some people even came to the house to try and persuade him. There were also girls who were interested in him, but he didn't want to get close to a girl.

"I won't ever get married, he said to me," Mrs Simpson told Aunty, "because it's meant for me to look after you. I'm happy the way things are."

And then Old Sunny Boy's old adoptive mother one day told Aunty some very distressing news, so that she came bursting into our house afterwards. She looked so upset that my mother gave her sugar water.

"What's the matter? Come tell me now!"

"No, I don't think that I should tell you, just now you get a shock and then I must struggle with you with an asthma attack," Aunty said.

"I'm fine! I promise I won't get an attack, just tell me," Mom insisted.

So Aunty explained, "Mrs Simpson got eviction papers from the Group Areas, and she doesn't yet know how to tell Old Sunny Boy. She has been allocated a house in a place called Lavender Hill. She says she never heard of a place by that name and doesn't even know where it is. It's a one-roomed house, and that means Old Sunny Boy will have to sleep in the lounge. Here he has a big room all to himself. She's worried sick, old Mrs Simpson says, not so much for herself but for her boy. He's going to miss his friends in District Six, and if they move it means that he'll have to travel far to work, whereas now he can walk there. It takes him less than fifteen minutes to get to work. He even comes home lunchtimes to check up on her."

For a moment Mom was stunned into silence. "Can you see what's happening here?" Aunty said to Mom. "Soon it will be your turn and what are you going to do?"

But my mother stayed calm. She didn't get an attack of asthma as Aunty had feared, she only said, "It's another sad day today. All we can do is wait to see what will happen."

"Well, I'd better make myself scarce. I don't want that husband of yours to find me here." And Aunty left.

Two days later, we received the news that Mrs Simpson had had a heart attack during the night and that she passed away in her sleep.

Old Sunny Boy was heartbroken. He blamed his old lady's death on the Group Areas. He said that if that man from the Department had not turned up at their house, then his old lady would not have died so suddenly. The shock was just too much for her. She was old and had lived all her life in District Six. She only knew the people from the District and now she was going to be sent to the outskirts of who-knows-where. She was better off dead in her home in District Six, he said, than in some strange place.

Old Sunny Boy made the arrangements for her funeral, which was attended by all who knew her. His insurance company sent a very big wreath. All the guys who always hung out at the shop with him also attended the funeral and with him sang a farewell to his mother.

Not long afterwards Old Sunny Boy stopped singing outside the shop because Mr Solly had also been given papers to leave. But Sunny did not leave straight away. After his old lady's funeral he stayed on in the house until he had sorted out all her belongings, most of which he gave away to neighbours and friends. His old lady had left him some money, and he had a bit saved up. He gave a month's notice at work, and we later heard that he left for Durban to see if he could join a group there and earn a living with his singing.

23 Mr Leonard and his primus stoves

I THINK THAT MR LEONARD was a bit deaf as he always placed his hand behind his one ear and pushed it towards the person speaking to him. He also had lots of grey hairs growing out of his ears.

Mr Leonard shared a house in Clyde Street with his wife. They had no children. Mr Leonard spoke with a strange accent. Nobody actually knew what nationality he was. Some people speculated that he was from Holland and others said that he was German, but nobody really cared – it was not important because he was a nice man. His wife was from up country, somewhere in the Albertinia district. She was frail and spoke only Afrikaans. She refused to speak English, because, she always said, she was a born Afrikaner. District Six was very cosmopolitan, so this never bothered anybody. As Mr Tahir Levy, a community worker in the olden days of District Six, still loves to say:

> We spoke Afrikaans
> We read English
> We recited Arabic and
> We sung Dutch

Mr Leonard was a wizard with a soldering iron and his speciality was repairing primus stoves. On one side of his backyard he had a workroom which was stacked with tattered primus stoves. Spare parts were lying in little heaps all over the cement floor. He never believed in throwing anything away because, he always said, "There might come a day when I may need it."

People came from all over District Six to his house in Clyde Street to have their primus stoves repaired. It was a full-time job and he made his living this way. Sometimes when people came from Athlone to do business in Cape Town, they too would leave their primus stove with Mr Leonard to fix. They dropped it off in the morning and collected it on their way home in the afternoon.

Mr Leonard was very fond of sherry, and usually he had a bottle stashed away in the workshop and had a tot whenever he felt like it. His wife did not approve of her husband's drinking, so he was not allowed to bring his bottle into the house. Sometimes my dad would pop in to see him and then the two of them would share a drink.

Mr Leonard was a very kind old man. People used to come to him and ask if they could buy a second-hand primus stove as they did not have enough money to buy a new one. To help them out he would allow them to make a small deposit and take a stove and then pay it off in instalments.

Often children were sent to Mr Leonard with broken primus stoves. Practically all the people in District Six were paid weekly. They would receive their pay on Friday and by Monday all their money would be spent or paid out. There were times when a primus stove broke during the week. Usually the children were then sent to Mr Leonard with the instruction to tell him that their mother said she couldn't come because she had to look after the little ones at home and if she came herself she would have to bring her whole brood with her.

But looking after the small children was only an excuse. The real reason was that there was no money to pay Mr Leonard straight away. He of course knew that people could only pay him on a Friday, so he would tell the children, as he handed the repaired stove back, to tell their mommy it cost two and six, or three shillings.

Sometimes if it only took him a minute to find the fault he would say, "Tell your daddy there was no charge, but he can send me some vegetables when he again gets a lot from his boss at the market in Sir Lowry Road."

Giving something in exchange was how some people paid Mr Leonard. When he fixed the shoemaker's stove, his shoes were repaired for free. An old Muslim lady would send him and his wife roti and curry, and on a Sunday the children from a family in Aspeling Street would often bring over a plate of hot koeksisters.

Mr Leonard never charged our family for any repairs as my dad always gave him a fair share of the crayfish and hottentot he caught at Oudekraal and Clifton Fourth Beach.

One day Mom complained to my father that the primus stove that Mr Leonard had just repaired was still not working properly. Dad tested the head with the small nipple key and could find nothing wrong. So he poured some methylated spirits in the little ring bowl at the base of the head and lit it with a match. He waited a few seconds for the head to get warm and then started to pump the stove. This pumping would create pressure in the brass container with paraffin at the bottom, the paraffin would spurt out the head and catch fire and so make the stove burn. The more you pumped the faster the stove burned.

But alas, our stove never got to burn faster – it exploded and burst open instead!

When we heard the big bang my mother and all of us stormed into the kitchen to see what had caused the noise. My dad was not burned or injured, but the primus stove was in pieces. Only then did Dad discover the reason why the stove would not burn: there was no paraffin in it!

We all considered it a big joke, except for my mother, who took it seriously.

"What if there'd been paraffin in it?" she said. "It could still have exploded and what then?" After that, she refused to ever have a primus stove in the house again. The primus stove was replaced with a gas cooker.

In the end, most of the people replaced their primus stoves with gas cookers. But for a different reason: there was no longer anybody to repair them. One Tuesday afternoon Mr Leonard came to tell my dad that he and his wife had received a visit from the Group Areas. They had been asked to produce their identity documents. When it was discovered that he was in fact a German immigrant and his wife a white boer-lady, they were told that they could no longer stay where they were.

"We have no intention of leaving District Six as my wife and I have been living here in this house in Clyde Street ever since the Second World War," he told them.

The man from the Group Areas told him that he was only doing his job and he was there to see that government orders were carried out.

"I love District Six and I and my wife have come to respect and love the people around us. We are part of the community," Mr Leonard told the official.

"Why don't you go back to Germany?" the official asked.

"Why would I go back there? When I was there all I thought about was to get out of the country because of what happened while I was there, all that persecution under Hitler. Now I see you want to do the same thing here with your damned forced removals."

The official had nothing to say to this. Then Mr Leonard said to Dad, like he had said to the official, "All the time my wife and I have lived in Clyde Street, we have been happy and contented."

The official only said, "If you do not move out within the given notice period of three months, we will come and move you personally."

"Mr Alex," old Mr Leonard said to Dad, "My wife and I are too old to put up a fight. My wife has come to love Cape Town so much that she has no intention of going back to live on the family farm up country. So I asked the official if we could be allocated a house out on the Cape Flats so that we can still be amongst the people of District Six. The man told me that number one, I am White and so is my wife, and number two, there is no guarantee that the people from District Six are all going to the same area. They will be moved to places like Manenberg, Bonteheuwel, Netreg, Lavender Hill, Retreat, Steenberg, Hanover Park and Belhar.

"Now, Mr Alex, I never heard half of those names of the places he mentioned!" The old man was really devastated. "I might just as well be dead," he said.

To calm him down, Dad took out a bottle of Old Brown Sherry. Mr Leonard left our house when the bottle was empty.

A few days later Mr Leonard came back to our house to inform my dad that he and his wife had decided to rent a flat in Green Point.

"What will you live on now?" my dad asked.

"I have a little bit saved up and my wife and I both get a pension."

Mr Leonard and his wife left and other people were temporarily housed in their old place in Clyde Street. Every Saturday Mr Leonard and his wife came back to visit their friends in District Six. They never went home empty-handed. And then after a while the old lady stopped coming with her husband because her legs were giving her trouble.

"It's those stairs at the flats that cause her so much pain. She misses District Six so much because everything is harder for her at the flat. The shops are a distance away and here in the old area there's a shop on every corner and never a shortage of children who she could ask to get something or do something for her," Mr Leonard said to Dad. "She has no friends in the flats as most of the people keep to themselves. Mrs Leonard does not feel like living any more."

After a while he, too, stopped making his trips. His wife had become sicker and he could not leave her alone. It was not very long before he came to tell us that she had passed away. He was heartbroken and soon came to say goodbye too us.

"I never mentioned it before, Mr Alex," he told Dad, "but I have a younger brother who owns a farm in the Transvaal. He settled there in 1950. When I told him about my wife's death, he said

I would be welcome to come and live with them. I have no option because I'm getting older and soon I won't be able to take care of myself. While I still have a little bit of strength to travel I might as well go."

The day Mr Leonard boarded the train at Cape Town Station was a sad day. Whoever came to see him off brought something for him. Mrs Kahn from our street sent her son with a large tin of home-made Malay biscuits and cookies. The man from the fish shop on the corner of Hanover and Longmarket Street gave him a large brown paper parcel with three salted snoek. "Fish is scarce in the Transvaal," he said.

My mother filled a large Consol preserve jar with pickled yellowtail and baked a loaf of bread for his long journey – yellowtail was the old man's favourite fish. Dad gave him a large jar of his special pickled crayfish tails, preserved in vinegar and spices.

"Old Leonard, my chum, when you eat this," he said, "don't forget to wash it down with a hearty shot of sherry. Here, this is to keep you warm on your long ride to the Transvaal." And he handed him a bottle of Old Brown Sherry.

Everybody said their farewells and good wishes and then to everyone's surprise, old Mr Leonard said, "Lebt wohl! Meine lieben Freunde, ich werde euch und District Six nie vergessen. Vielen Dank für alle eure Liebe und Herzlichkeit gegenüber mir und meiner Frau."*

Then I heard my dad whispering, half to himself, "So old Leonard was German all the time, just like I suspected. With a name like Leonard, I always wondered if it was his real name. Poor old chap, at least he knows where he's going."

---

* Farewell, my beloved friends, I will never forget you or District Six. Thank you for all your love and kindness to me and my wife.

24 Mrs Salie the hawker lady

EVERY SATURDAY MRS SALIE turned up with her horse and cart, stacked high with fresh fruit and vegetables. She was smart and real businesslike and only sold the best. Everybody knew that the corner of Tyne and Hanover Streets was her corner. This was an unspoken rule and no-one ever invaded her space on a Saturday morning because she was a woman that was scared of no-one.

Mrs Salie always wore expensive clothes, with over them a white coat, which was always open. Her large hawker's badge was displayed on the coat.

All hawkers had to wear a white coat and display a badge. If the Law spotted someone selling fruit and vegetables without a licence they would confiscate their goods and sometimes even throw the hawker in the police van. Many times the "illegal" hawker would leave his waentjie and run and hide. Often the Law then took his cart and goods away. At other times, naughty children would steal the fruit and vegetables while the police were busy chasing the hawker.

When the Law checked up on Mrs Salie they could never find anything wrong, and yet they always wanted things for free.

Mrs Salie kept her paper money in her bra, and the small change she kept in her coat pocket. Her mouth was full of gold teeth and she wore masses of gold bangles on her arms, and each time she reached into her pocket they would jingle.

Some Saturday mornings I asked my mom if I could help Mrs Salie. I liked to listen to her because she had many different ways of speaking. When one of the white shop assistants from Van der Schyff's dress material shop came out to buy from her, she would say, "Good morning, madam. To what do I owe the pleasure of you visiting me on this beautiful day?"

If the assistant made a purchase of maybe just one item, Mrs Salie would continue unashamedly, "But madam, how about some lovely red apples, just like the colour of your cheeks? Or some first grade oranges and naartjies to keep that cold away? And oh madam, you must buy some of these grapes!"

With compliments like these, people could not resist to buy from her. When the assistant had bought enough to fill a tomato box Mrs Salie would shout, "Hey, Achmat, don't sit and sleep, come, come, man, there's a delivery to be made. Here, carry the madam's goods into the shop for her."

Achmat would jump to attention saying, "Yes, yes, Mrs Salie, coming right up and at your service, madam."

Achmat was a colourful character and he never took offence, no matter what people said to him. When he and the customer left, Mrs Salie would say, "A person must work bloody hard to sell fruit and vegetables. It's the people that have money that's so stingy to buy!"

A few minutes later a dirty, drunk skollie would pass and request some old veggies and fruit. He'd say, "Ag please, merem, isn't there perhaps a old groenetjie to keep the pot going? Merem knows how it goes, I got no money."

This would really put Mrs Salie in a temper. She'd get very angry and yell at him, "You want to tell me that you got no money, you drunken sod, you should be ashamed of yourself, your wife and children are waiting for you at home, and look at you!" She would reach for the long whip that was always close by and threaten him. She never hit anybody, but she had to show him "and his sort" that they should not mess with her. Then she would shout after him, "A damned cheek to tell me he got no money. Where did he get money for wine?"

The drunkard would stagger away, mumbling, "Shoo, but that merem is kwaai. I better go before she use that whip on me. Goobye, merempie, so long and have a good time."

Mrs Salie was not a stingy person. If a child came up to buy an apple and he only had one penny or cent to pay for it and maybe it cost three, then she would not send him away. Instead she would give him two apples that were not so perfect and maybe a banana that was slightly bruised, and the child would be only too happy to part with his coins.

Mrs Sophia was one of Mrs Salie's regular customers. She was poor and lived in a house in Rotten Row, just off Parkin Street. She had very little money, but her worn old clothes were always neat and clean. Over the faded dresses she used to wear a freshly washed and ironed apron, and on her head she wore a scarf. Her one luxury was to wear stockings. She never left the house without stockings on, even if she was wearing slippers. And she was very fond of her blue felt slippers with tan pom-poms! She also never left home without her black leather sakkie. She never used any makeup, but her face would shine from the Vaseline that she rubbed on.

Mrs Sophia was a soft-spoken woman who slaved all her married life for her eight children, including two sets of twins. All the children were still at school. Her husband worked for a car dealer with a showroom down in Roeland Street, opposite the Kimberley Hotel. His earnings were just not enough, so Mrs Sophia took in washing and ironing to increase the family income.

Mrs Salie liked respectable, hardworking people. After Mrs Sophia paid for her goods, Mrs Salie sometimes gave her a handful of loose carrots and a cauliflower that had been slightly damaged in the packing. And if there was bruised fruit available, that too would be packed into the black leather sakkie.

Mrs Sophia might be poor, but she was very proud and always refused to take things for free.

114

Mrs Salie insisted, "You are one of my best customers! Come rain or shine, every Saturday morning you come and buy from me. So please accept this as a gift." She was holding out one of the best quality juicy mangoes.

Mrs Sophia could not resist the temptation.

"Enjoy it all by yourself when you have a quiet moment!" Mrs Salie said as she handed the fruit to her.

Mrs Sophia thanked the hawker lady most humbly. After she left, Mrs Salie would turn to me and say, "See, Penny, a person must do good as that is where your blessings lie. I can't just dish my stuff out to any Tom, Dick and Harry, but I give to those who deserve it."

Mrs Salie spent all Saturday morning and most of the afternoon at her stand. I often wondered when she found the time to eat and where she went to the toilet! When it quietened a bit she would draw up a wooden box and count her money. Each time she separated the paper money from the change and put it in its special, unmentionable place. The horse was fed and watered and Achmat would doze off under the cart.

I enjoyed being in the company of Mrs Salie. Mom knew where I was but my dad never suspected. Had he ever found out that I was helping Mrs Salie, he would certainly have stopped me from going there again. He believed that it was not proper for a girl to be standing on a street corner selling fruit and vegetables. So if he happened to look for me, Mom would quickly send one of the younger children to call me and I would appear in less than two minutes. If Dad asked where I had been, I would tell him that I was playing in Roger Street.

Mrs Salie did not mind that I occasionally ran away from her corner like this as I was just "freelancing", and she could pay me whatever she wanted. But, in fact, the money was not very important to me, because it was fun working for her, plus it gave me the opportunity to get out of the crowded house and out of having to do housework.

For many years Mrs Salie continued to come to her corner on Saturday mornings. With time she aged, I was grown up now and went to work, but I often still passed her stand for a chat or to buy some fruit. And then she too disappeared. Like so many things in District Six, Mrs Salie's Saturday morning visits on the corner were suddenly a thing of the past. Shrand's had a clearance sale and the shoe shop was closed. The same happened to Van der Schyff's dress material shop.

People outside District Six didn't realise what was happening and months afterwards people still came from all over to get material for special occasions, or shoes, only to discover that they had come in vain.

When I didn't see her anymore, I went to visit Mrs Salie in her house in Aspeling Street. It was a beautiful place, but she was packing up because they were moving to Primrose Park.

"They offered us a council house in Steenberg, but we refused to take it," she said. "So we bought our own."

Just as I was about to leave, she asked me to wait a moment. She returned with two of her gold bangles.

"Here, take this, Penny. I'm old and have no use for these any longer. The others I have already given to my two daughters."

When I hesitated, she said, "Just see that you come and visit us in Primrose Park!"

25 Dad departs

I T WAS EARLY MARCH 1971. I was working as a receptionist for an insurance brokers' firm in Strand Street. This particular day I took a leisurely walk home after work. I sauntered down Strand Street, across the Parade and into Darling Street. I passed Castle Bridge and crossed into Hanover Street. By now three shops had closed down. The windows and doorways were closed up with sheets of corrugated iron. The whole street looked abandoned.

I went through Rotten Row and into Parkin Street which led me right into Tyne Street. I was glad to be home because it was an extremely hot afternoon. There wasn't a breath of wind.

Table Mountain, flanked by Devil's Peak and Lion's Head, stood contented, keeping watch over the city. The sky was a hazy blue. In District Six a late summer atmosphere prevailed. Many people were relaxing outside their houses, while groups of children played in the streets.

On entering the house, I saw Dad dressed in thick winter pyjamas. I could not understand it.

"Your father insists that he is getting cold," my mother said.

"Cold?" I replied. "But Mom, it's unbearably hot."

Mom said that she had had the doctor in to examine him and that he could not find anything wrong.

When Ron came home from work he asked me if I want to go with him and his girlfriend to the Goodwood Drive-In.

"Me go to the drive-in?" I said. "You know that I'm not as fair as you and Susan. They will throw me out, or they won't let me in. They'll just allow the two of you in and I'll be left standing outside. No thanks. Ron."

As I worked and started to move outside District Six, I had

become more and more aware of the apartheid laws that were being enforced. Inside the District the colour of one's skin never counted. At work we had to use separate toilet facilities; there was hardly any eating place in town where we could now sit down and have a meal. At the railway station we suddenly had to use a separate entrance. The same applied to the subways. At each station there was a subway for whites and one for "non-whites". The railway ticket boxes, the buses and trains, the post office, the hospitals – everything was segregated. So I had become very sensitive about my "race classification".

But Ron insisted and finally I agreed to go.

When I told Dad that I was going, he begged me to stay with him. Mom consoled him, saying that she and the other children would be there.

We had no problem at the drive-in and I made up my mind that in the future I would go into other white theatres and bioscopes with Ron and Susan. And I did, and as Ron had predicted, "No genuine white would interfere with you here in Cape Town. It takes a Coloured to recognise a Coloured and cause trouble."

I never had any problems because I was not white.

But that was later.

When we returned from the drive-in that evening, Mom told us that Dad had kept my brother Pete sitting at his bedside for a long time while he talked about his days in the Second World War. The old photos and General Smuts's letter had been taken out and Dad had relived his army days once more.

Dad was a difficult man all his life and sometimes we wondered whether the war had something to do with it, because in his letter to ex-servicemen General Smuts had written:

The aftermath of war and the process of readjustment are likely to produce many difficulties and problems. Patience

118

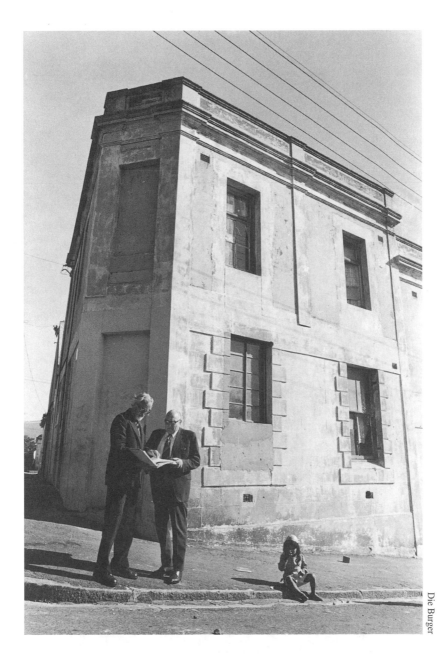

Die Burger

As late as August 1979, some concerned individuals tried to prevent the demolition of the few achitectural treasures still standing. Here, Prof. J J Oberholster (right), the then Director of the National Monuments Council, discusses the possibility of saving the corner double-storey at Upper Ashley and Upper Sheppard Streets.

Die Burger

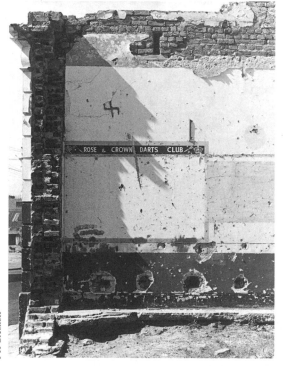

J H Greshoff

Above: By the end of May 1975, Barney's Paint & Hardware and The Little Wonder Store could be viewed from a distance for the first time – because that is when the bulldozers reached Hanover Street. Like the name suggests, The Little Wonder Store sold just about everything, but what 82-year-old Mrs Stern, one of the many Jewish shop-owners in the old District Six, remembers best today, is the yards and yards of curtaining she sold to house-proud housewives.

The Rose & Crown on the corner of Tennant and Hanover Streets, and favourite bar of the author's father, among others, also succumbed to the bulldozers. The destruction of the building, still in relatively good shape, was particularly sad.

J H Greshoff

As children the author and her sisters had to wait their turn on the swings in the big play park on Rutger Street. The place, one of the very few open areas in the District put aside for children, was always crowded with youngsters impatient to get rid of their excess energy.

Next page: The Seven Steps, "headquarters" of the Seven Steps Gang in the good old days of District Six (or bad, depending how you look at it), lie deserted and forlorn after the houses, streets and lanes, around them, which once offered shelter from the "Law", had been destroyed. The only improvement was the unobstructed view of Table Mountain that could now be enjoyed!

Noor Ebrahim

and tolerance will be needed and the demands upon your courage and spirit of service will remain as great as ever ...

It must have been about two o'clock that night when I was awakened by noises coming from my parents' room. I got up. Mom was still fully dressed.

I ran and woke Ron. Together we rushed down the long passage to our parents' room. When he saw Dad, Ron got a fright. In no time he had rushed him to Woodstock Hospital in his car.

Mom and Ron arrived back from the hospital at half past four. They reported that Dad had been admitted and examined straight away and that tests would be carried out as soon as the day shift started. The sister in charge had asked Mom if we had a telephone.

"No, we have no phone," she said, "but our neighbour across the road won't mind if we give her phone number."

We tried to sleep.

It was hardly light, when someone knocked on our front door. I answered. It was Mrs Adams.

"Come quickly," she said, "the sister at Woodstock Hospital is on the phone. You have to go at once."

Ron and I went. We left Mom to sleep but woke Shirley up. She would tell Mom we had gone back to the hospital.

Dad's eyes were closed. He had a hint of a smile on his face. We spoke to him, but the doctor said that he was sleeping and could not hear us. His heart had weakened, but the test results would only be available later.

The doctor returned later and urged me to go home.

I walked all the way home. When I got there it was eight-thirty. Shirley had left for work and the five younger children had gone to their different schools. Mom was on her way to the hospital.

I arrived late at work and could not concentrate on anything.

119

Mid-morning I received a phone call from Dave, Ron's best friend. "Penny, my deepest sympathy," he said.

"Deepest sympathy?" I repeated. But I already knew that Dad had passed away.

His death certificate read: "Cardiac failure".

As soon as our neighbours and friends heard about Dad's death they came over to our house. They came not only from Tyne Street, but also from Parkin, Roger, Aspeling and Godfrey Streets. Mrs Adams from across the road sent a two-kilogram pack of sugar and two tins of condensed milk. Aunty Lettie sent some koeksisters and Mrs Kahn a packet of assorted biscuits. Kika sent a big packet of Five Roses tea. Motjie Awa and Boeta Bruima sent money wrapped up in a piece of newspaper, and Mrs Kader on the corner promised my mother that she would make a big pot of mutton curry for the funeral.

This was not unusual as the people of Tyne Street, as all over in the District, always stood by one another.

When Dad was alive he expressed the wish to be buried from home. So on the eve of his funeral his body was brought to the house. He was laid out in the coffin which was placed on two chairs in the front room. There was a large arrangement of flowers on a side table and the curtains were drawn.

When I went up to Holy Cross Primary School in Nile Street earlier that day to fetch Daisy and Colin, one of the nuns gave me a bottle of holy water. Aunty (she could be very supportive at times!) now sprinkled some of it in and around the coffin.

Neighbours and friends poured in to pay their last respects. Part of the coffin was left open so that they could see Dad's face. He was clean-shaven and his hair was neatly brushed. Some neighbours said that he made a very good-looking corpse.

Then a young man in his early twenties unexpectedly turned up at the house. We had not seen Ricky for about six years. We were all extremely pleased to see him because he was one of the young boys that often went fishing with Dad.

"What made you decide to come and visit us this evening?" Mom asked him when we had gotten over the surprise.

"I had to come to you today because of Uncle Alex's passing away."

"Did you see the death notice in the newspaper?"

"No, Aunty Jean, I didn't read about it, I found it out rather by chance. I work for Goodall & Williams, your undertaking firm. I saw Uncle Alex's name on a form and recognised it. So I went to the morgue to see if it was indeed Uncle Alex. I got a big shock when I pulled out the big drawer and looked in his face. I didn't expect I'd come face to face with him in this way. It was always my plan to visit him here in Tyne Street."

We couldn't help but smile.

"That was when I decided to go to my boss and ask if he'd allow me to arrange the funeral. He agreed immediately."

We all felt better that someone we knew would be taking care of the arrangements. We, the children, had never experienced a death in our immediate family, so this was the first funeral of our generation.

The day of the funeral was very hot. As Dad had wished, the funeral was conducted from home. Father Thornton from the Holy Cross Church led the funeral service. The house was too small to hold the neighbours and friends and many of them had to stand outside in the street. When the service was over, we queued to have the last chance to see Dad's face.

All of us girls placed a carnation in the coffin because Mom said it was his favourite flower. Then Mom bent down and kissed Dad's cold forehead. We followed her example, and then the other people paid their final respects. The coffin was closed and wheeled away and placed inside the hearse.

Dad was buried in Maitland Cemetery, near Gate Ten in Voortrekker Road. Father Thornton held a short service and we sang Psalm 23, "The Lord is my shepherd", at the graveside.

After the funeral, the family and friends came back to our house, the older people to drink tea and the younger ones to enjoy some Pepsi Cola. Dora, who sometimes helped Mom in the house, had prepared a table in the front room while we were away. She had already put out all the food that had been given to us – the mutton curry and rice, some samoosas and sandwiches, biscuits and koeksisters.

By six that evening everybody was gone. The atmosphere in the house was strange and different. Dad had always been with us, his passing away at fifty-one came unexpectedly. Mom suddenly had to face the uncertain future with her eight children all by herself.

26 First experience with a bulldozer

THERE WERE MANY PEOPLE IN District Six who did not even know that a word like "bulldozer" existed. Most of them had never seen such a thing, not even on a picture.

Our first encounter with a bulldozer was terrifying. Suddenly one morning this big monstrosity rumbles and roars down Tyne Street and comes to an abrupt halt in Chapel Street.

Most of the neighbours and their children were running behind it, while other grown-ups had gathered outside their homes to see what the noise was all about. It looked as if a space ship had just landed, as if it had come to invade District Six.

"Can you people now see what's happening here? I told you the world is coming to an end!" one old lady shouted.

"No!" a man shouted back from across the street. "The world is not coming to an end, we here in District Six are coming to an end!"

The driver of the bulldozer shouted at the people to make way for him as he had a job to do.

"I was sent to demolish the cooldrink factory," he tried to explain. "Isn't this it?" he asked, pointing at the old building near the Sidney Street corner. "Now please, get out of the way! People who get in the way will get hurt!"

Slowly the people moved away.

"Oh," an old man whom I had often seen shuffling along with his walking stick moaned, "I'm so glad that my wife didn't live long enough to witness what is happening here today. We lived here for sixty years. Sixty years! All gone." And slowly he walked away.

As the bulldozer rammed it, the building started falling apart bit by bit. First one wall, then a next. Then part of the roof tumbled in.

The bulldozer just kept going like a huge war tank.

My younger sister Patsy had covered her ears because the noise of bricks and timber and iron being torn apart was unbearable.

"No, go away!" she screamed. "Stop, stop!"

But her small child's pleas were lost in the sounds of destruction.

Most people stood as if they had just received an electric shock. Speechless they gazed at the destruction in front of them. Daisy clung to Mom, petrified that our house would be next.

"I wish I had a gun like John Wayne so that I could shoot that guy on the bulldozer," Pete hissed. Mom's reply could not be heard as another wall crashed noisily to the ground.

Boeta Bruima had his arms round Motjie Awa. She was sobbing softly, tears running down her wrinkled brown cheeks. He didn't try to console her, he just shook his head from side to side.

After a while we could hardly see. Clouds of dust rose from the rubble. Faintly one could see waterpipes and electric wires standing out like bloodless veins amongst the debris.

Not long after the bulldozer, a cartage contractor arrived to cart the demolished cooldrink factory away. And as soon as the last broken bricks and chunks of cement were taken away, another contractor arrived with a loader truck and started to dig a huge hole where the factory used to stand.

This puzzled the bystanders, and a little boy asked the driver why he was making such a big hole.

"Can't tell you," the man answered, "can just tell you that the next building to go will be the Rose & Crown Bar in Hanover Street." He laughed.

"Why the Rose & Crown? It's still a smart building and people use it," one of the regulars of the bar objected.

"Don't know why," the driver said, "but can everybody please move away so I can get on with my work!"

Nobody moved. Everybody went on watching. A rumour had started to go round that the Rose & Crown was going to be buried in that hole. It made the people even more upset.

One of the women who lived right next to the cooldrink factory said to the driver that leaving such a big hole open would be dangerous with all the small children around.

"Madam, it won't be long before all you people will be gone

too, so don't worry about the empty hole. There won't be any children to play in it," the driver replied, and he laughed again.

27   The last few months

R ON AND SUSAN GOT MARRIED in July 1971, in the middle of winter. We were all dressed in thick clothing as we went into St Mary's Cathedral at the bottom end of Roeland Street, just across from the Houses of Parliament. Shirley was bridesmaid and Ron's friend Dave was best man.

After the wedding ceremony, the newly married couple, their train, the families on both sides and some guests went to the old Company Gardens in the centre of town to have the wedding photographs taken. Afterwards there was a reception at a private clubhouse in Woodstock. It was a big wedding, with about 150 guests, and it was as happy an occasion as we could have had so soon after Dad's passing away.

The wedding couple spent their honeymoon in Mossel Bay. When they returned, they moved in with Susan's mother in Kensington, near Maitland.

Within a few months Mom had lost her husband and now her oldest son had moved away. She was left with seven children to take care of in a District that was becoming more and more deserted and unrecognisable. People were leaving every week. More and more buildings were being knocked down or closed up.

We missed a man in the house. Before Dad's death Mom never went out. That had now changed. She was forced to go out. Especially after Ron left the house.

I often thought of what Mr O'Connell said when he paid his last respects to Dad: "Alex, things are really getting bad here in District Six, lots of houses are already empty. It's a pity that you had to leave your family when they're going to need you most."

When I came home from work one afternoon in October that year, Mom told me that she had had no option but to fill in some forms.

It reminded me that by mistake I had left my beautiful maroon fountain pen with gold trimmings and my initials engraved on the side, at home that morning. I had missed it only when I got to work.

"Mom, have you perhaps seen my pen?" I asked.

She was embarrassed. The white official from the Group Areas who brought the forms to the house, she told me, saw my pen on the table and persuaded her to give it to him. "Penny, I said I could not as it was my daughter's pen and it was a very special gift. But he said if I give him the pen he'll see to it that we get a nice house."

"Mom, that man had no right to bribe you. I'm not going to move anywhere, and I'm going to find out who his superiors are and report him. You'll see, in the end that pen will make no difference!"

The man had clearly intimidated my mother, saying that if she did not sign the papers and move out as instructed, then he would have to make the necessary arrangements to forcibly remove us.

He needn't have told her. We knew that. We saw the government trucks every time they roared into what was still left of District Six.

"I want no more trouble, Penny. We have no choice. We don't have money for a deposit to buy a house. We have to move soon, whether we like it or not," Mom said.

"If Dad was alive he would've put up a fight," I insisted.

126

She was quiet for a while. Then she said, "You know, I think it's perhaps better that your father is no longer with us. You know how outspoken he was and not scared of anybody. We might have had more trouble if they threw him in jail."

So in her own way Mom did try to resist, but she was forced to accept the house that was allocated to us because of the responsibility she felt towards her children.

That night she called us all together and said that we would be leaving Tyne Street. We were moving to Hanover Park.

Time was drawing close. It had turned November and the official from the Group Areas once again came to ask if they could send a truck to remove us.

"No," my mother said. "Under no circumstances will we be seen leaving this place in one of your trucks. We will make our own arrangements when it is time to move."

"When do you intend moving?" he asked.

"You and your people will have to wait till the school-going children have completed their December exams," she said. "What's your rush? This place is going nowhere and the ground in District Six is going to lie empty for many years to come."

The man looked puzzled.

"Just wait and one day you'll understand what I mean!" she said.

Tension was running high in the house. The other children kept mentioning how they were going to miss their window-shopping trips, the walks on summer nights down Darling and Plein and Adderley Streets and up through the Gardens; the visits to the art gallery, the hothouse and the museum.

"What about our church?" they asked. There was no church in Hanover Park; the nearest Catholic Church was in Lansdowne.

At last the younger children finished their exams and the day arrived that one of Ron's friends came with his lorry. Everybody helped to carry the furniture out. We had to leave behind a solid embuia table because it would not fit into the new house. We also had to leave our big black Dover stove and a hall stand. We phoned Uncle Peter to collect these things.

Finally the lorry was loaded. All Ron's friends were there to go along and help carry the furniture into the house in Hanover Park.

"Uncle" Dan with Shirley and Penny shortly before
they left Tyne Street

I was the last one to leave the old house in Tyne Street. I lingered and could not get myself to walk out the front door. I went from room to room, feeling quite sick.

"Penny!" someone called.

"I'm looking for the cat," I replied. Meanwhile I was holding Sweety, the stray cat I found after Blackie died, in my arms.

Eventually I walked down the passage and out the front door.

It was not necessary to lock the front door. The house was going to be demolished and Uncle Peter was already on his way to collect the things that were left inside. I didn't even bother to pull the door closed. Number 14 would exist no more, nor would Aspeling, Godfrey or Parkin Streets.

I started to cry. I sobbed as if someone had just died. I didn't care, I was sentimental about District Six. The place was our home, after all.

Someone, I don't even remember who, came and comforted me. She wanted to know what the matter was.

"The cat scratched me," I said.

"It's okay, Penny," Mrs Adams said from across the street. "We all know how you feel because we all have one pain."

Then a passer-by observed, "If you remove a cat from familiar surroundings and you rub a little butter on its paws when it reaches its new destination, it will get accustomed to its new home very quickly."

Oh, I wish it was so simple, I thought.

End

IT WASN'T THAT SIMPLE.

After twenty-five years most of the ground in the former District Six still largely lies bare. I have often thought that maybe my mother knew something we didn't know when she spoke to the Group Areas official that day.

She died in Hanover Park in March 1988. Aunty, who moved back in with us after we left District Six, died there more than ten years before her, in August 1975.

The two of them would often sit on the modern couch in the lounge of the Hanover Park house with its matching walls and carpet, so different from the old bed-sitter at number 14 Tyne Street, and wonder what had happened to everybody.

Now that apartheid has been abolished and people are free to live where they choose, we children find ourselves scattered all over the Cape Peninsula: Parow North, Hout Bay, Ottery, Mitchell's Plain, Dieprivier, Mandalay.

I am the only one fortunate enough to work on the outskirts of what used to be District Six, doing what I love best: keeping alive, not just my own but also other people's memories of the place we used to love. For in December 1994 the District Six Museum was opened in the old Central Methodist Church in Buitekant Street, and soon afterwards I was employed as education officer.

List of un-English words

aapstert – literally, monkey's tail: whip

babbie – Indian male shopkeeper

babbie shop – Indian shop

bakkie – small truck

boer – here: white Afrikaans-speaking person

boeta – literally, brother: way of addressing an older, well-respected man, often unrelated to you

dagga – marijuana/*Cannabis sativa*

dennebolpitjietyd – pine-kernel season

dhaltjies – chilli bites

drie blikkies – children's game played with three tins

Eid – celebration at the end of the month-long fast of Ramadan observed by Muslims

goggas – insects

groenetjie – literally, small green one: vegetable

halaal – meat from animals slaughtered according to Muslim custom

handelaar – shopkeeper

kennetjie – game involving a short wooden peg and a long, straight stick

kerem – board game in which a stick is used to shoot disks into holes

kitke – plaited egg loaf, traditionally Jewish

koeksister – traditional Cape confection: deep-fried plaited piece of dough soaked in syrup

konfyt – jam

kroes kop – frizzy hair

kwaai – bad tempered; harsh

mebos – confection of salted and sugared dried apricots

mense van buite – people from outside

mieliemeel – maize meal

mos – untranslatable word used for emphasis: indeed, in fact

motjie – Indian lady shopkeeper

naartjie – tanjerine or mandarin orange

rooikop – literally, red head: red hair

roti/rooti – flat, round bread cooked on a flat surface

sakkie – small bag

samosa/samoosa – small, fried pastry triangle stuffed with curried meat or vegetables

sari – traditional dress of Indian women, consisting of a long, straight piece of cloth swathed around the body

sjambok – stout whip made from leather

skollie – member of a street gang; hooligan

smeer (with water melon) – to rub (someone else playfully with the white fleshy part just inside the outer skin)

smoorsnoek – flaked cooked snoek, braised with onions, diced cooked potato, tomatoes and chillies

snoekmootjies – pieces of raw snoek preserved in vinegar and spices

stinkvis – literally, stinking fish

stoep – porch, verandah

Tweede Nuwe Jaar – literally, Second New Year: second of January, a public holiday in the Cape

volop – plentiful

waentjie – hand-drawn cart

zoll – hand-rolled (dagga) cigarette